Silent

BUT

Deadly

Silent but Deadly

The Underlying Cultural Patterns of Everyday Behaviour

Kirsten Bell

CAW PRESS
London

Copyright © Kirsten Bell 2022
All rights reserved

A CIP catalogue record for this title is available from
the British Library

'Vintage cloud drawing' by OnlyGFX.com,
'Spider Web' by j4p4n, 'Family Sofa' by SVGRepo,
and 'Lemon Bird' font by Ian Barnard have been
reproduced under a CC-BY license

All other images, and the excerpt from 'The Spider and
the Fly' by Mary Howitt, are in the public domain

ISBN: 978-1-3999-3632-3

www.cawpress.com

*This book is dedicated to Bruce Kapferer.
I'd like to say that everything I learned
about the value of anthropology, I learned
from him, but I'm pretty sure he doesn't
want the blame for this book.*

CONTENTS

Preface

'Will you walk into my parlour?'
said the Spider to the Fly,
'Tis the prettiest little parlour
that ever you did spy;
The way into my parlour
is up a winding stair,
And I have many curious things
to shew when you are there.'
'Oh no, no,' said the little Fly,
'to ask me is in vain,
For who goes up your winding stair
can ne'er come down again.'

—Mary Howitt, 'The Spider and the Fly'

I decided to be an anthropologist when I was twelve years old. I can't remember exactly what prompted this desire, because anthropology is not a widely known discipline in Australia,* but I have a feeling that a 1988 horror movie, *The Serpent and the Rainbow*, is the culprit. Broadly inspired by a book by the ethnobotanist Wade Davis, the film is about a Harvard anthropologist who goes to Haiti to investigate a drug used to create zombies in Vodou rituals. I don't remember that much about it, beyond the protagonist being creatively tortured (nails and scrotums are involved) and then buried alive with a tarantula, except that

---

*I have been asked more than once whether anthropology is the study of ants.

i

it alerted me that it was possible to have a job studying other cultures. At the time, I was an avid devourer of books on 'voodoo', witchcraft, ancient civilizations, the Bermuda Triangle, and other unexplained phenomena, so the idea of getting paid to study these sorts of topics for a living was deeply alluring. Basically, I became an anthropologist for all the wrong reasons: its exotic appeal and the idea of studying strange beliefs in foreign lands.

When I got to university, I was quickly set to rights about the nature of anthropology, which has long tried to distance itself from the widespread view of the discipline as a purveyor of the exotic and handmaiden of European colonialism. An oft-reproduced characterization of anthropology is that it strives to 'make the strange familiar and the familiar strange'. Although of uncertain vintage, the enduring popularity of this expression stems from its rare distinction of being an aphorism that is both catchy *and* true. However, while I was attracted to anthropology because I sought out the strange and the curious, it was the familiar and the mundane that soon fascinated me. During my doctoral fieldwork in South Korea in the late 1990s, my fieldnote books were crammed not only with information about the religion I was studying but detailed descriptions of television ads for hygiene products, rules around dining etiquette, and what happened on the rare occasions I saw someone fart.

Once I finished my doctorate, I began the first of various intercontinental moves: to the USA in 2000, where I had spent time as a child, then back to Australia in 2003 (with some field trips to Korea in between), then to Canada in 2006, and most recently to the UK in 2018. Unlike South Korea, where I expected to be confronted with cultural differences, I was less prepared for them in the lands of my Anglophone brethren. It wasn't just accents, idioms, and expletives that caused problems; familiar spaces became fraught, and rituals had to be acquired (or relearned). Despite being an anthropologist, and a so-called expert on culture, I was constantly committing faux pas: stiffing my hairdresser on tips in Canada, embarrassing my hairdresser in London by insisting on tipping her, amusing Americans by swearing, offending Canadians by swearing, confirming Brits' stereotypes about Australians by swearing. I went from having good teeth in Australia to bad teeth in Canada to great teeth in the UK, and my washing machine went from a utility room in Sydney to a cupboard in Vancouver to the kitchen in London.

My goal in this book is to share the anthropological insights I have gleaned from the sometimes bewildering differences I saw between the five countries I have lived in and my long history of committing blatant cultural gaffes.* Although it has become somewhat unfashionable in anthropology to talk of culture, it is the central preoccupation of this book. My favourite articulation of the concept comes from the American anthropologist Clifford Geertz, who once said that 'man is an animal suspended in webs of significance he himself has spun, I take culture to be those webs'. For Geertz, the anthropologist's job was to articulate and interpret the webs of meaning in which we are ensnared—webs that have a distinct shape and feel from culture to culture, even if the general outlines are similar. In a somewhat different metaphor, the anthropologist Gillian Tett likens the role of the anthropologist to that of a radiologist. In her words, 'anthropologists use an

---

*In light of this history, you may have some understandable doubts about my prowess as an anthropologist, but rest assured that the burned hand teaches best.†

†See what I mean about aphorisms?

X-ray machine to look at society, to see half-hidden patterns we are only dimly aware of. This often shows us that even if we think "x" is the reason why something has happened, it might actually be "y"'. As I aim to show, almost everything we think about why we do the things we do is, at best, partially right and, at worst, completely wrong.

In writing this book, I am breaking an unwritten taboo in anthropology, which is that the public is the subject of our work but rarely its audience. If you pick up a popular anthropology book, you can almost guarantee that it's not written by an anthropologist. In fact, some of the writers most associated with anthropology are from other fields: Jared Diamond is a physiologist, ornithologist, and geographer;* Yuval Noah Harari is a historian; Wade Davis is an ethnobotanist. There are some notable exceptions, including Kate Fox, the author of *Watching the English*, and Gillian Tett, the author of *Anthro-Vision*, but it's a sad truth that many contemporary anthropologists are reluctant to engage with the public. This wasn't always the case. Sir James Frazer's *The Golden Bough*, published in 1890, was widely read by a scandalized British public, and anthropologists like Franz Boas and Margaret Mead had a vibrant public presence in the USA. The French anthropologist Claude Lévi-Strauss was a leading intellectual in post-war France, and something of a global academic celebrity to boot.**

---

*Although he does make the average academic look undertrained.

**My undergraduate lecturer Douglas Miles once entertained students with an account of Lévi-Strauss turning up in San Francisco when Levi Strauss & Co, the maker of Levi's jeans, was celebrating its anniversary, and assuming the parade was for him. The story was probably the product of Doug's irreverent sense of humour, but I nevertheless like to picture Lévi-Strauss waving to the bemused masses from his vehicle to a chorus of bewildered exclamations of 'Who *was* that guy?'

In recent years, anthropologists seem to have mostly become allergic to straightforward, accessible prose, which is associated with 'dumbing down' our ideas, themselves considered far too complex and nuanced to expose them to—heaven forbid!—lay interpretations.* These attitudes are so entrenched that Tett includes a postscript at the end of *Anthro-Vision* for anthropologists, acknowledging that some may find her 'depiction of their prized concepts and methodology simplistic' but that her goal is to see anthropological ideas more widely taken up. Fox takes a more combative approach to the anthropological purists in the newest edition of *Watching the English.* 'I make no apology for my continued refusal... to pander to this stuffy minority by trying to show off my comprehensive reading, command of fancy jargon, mastery of abstruse concepts, ability to obfuscate simple ones, and all the other stuff that might make the book more palatable to them', she writes.

That said, stepping outside of scholarly comfort zones can be perilous, which is one of the more valid reasons for anthropologists' reluctance to engage with the public. I learned this the hard way in 2012 when a reporter got in

---

*Even the use of PowerPoint was initially frowned upon for this reason, which I learned after I presented my first paper at an anthropology conference in 1997. Having never presented at a conference, I approached my older sister, a geologist, for advice. 'Use PowerPoint,' she told me; 'everyone's doing it.' She even provided her own personalized template (blue background with yellow writing—fashionable amongst scientists in the mid 1990s and heartily despised by the time it finally went out of fashion a decade later). The conference paper was a complete failure. While my unfortunate mispronunciation of the word 'cacophony'† didn't help matters, the academic who chaired the session politely but pointedly informed me afterwards that while the use of PowerPoint might be *de rigueur* in scientific circles, it wasn't at all the thing amongst anthropologists, as our complex and abstract musings didn't lend themselves well to bullet points on a slide.

†Not *cack*-oh-fanny, as it turns out, but the counter-intuitive cack-*off*-ony.

touch asking if I could offer some comments for an article she was writing about the unveiling of the iPad Mini. The reporter was looking for an anthropologist willing to provide some 'light-hearted and fun' observations on the culture of Apple product launches, and I quite liked the idea of poking some gentle fun at Apple and its acolytes, who tend to be rather zealous in their affection.* I agreed to prepare some comments for her, which amounted to watching a couple of Apple launches on YouTube, reading a few academic articles, and putting together some observations that met the brief I'd been given. The religious parallels are so obvious (albeit superficial) that it's impossible not to draw them, so I discussed revivals, sacred symbols, origins myths, and the like. However, the reporter then asked if we could have a follow-up phone conversation so she could ask some 'more academic questions'. Although a little worried that she seemed to be treating my 'light-hearted' comments with an undue degree of seriousness, I reluctantly agreed. 'How could it hurt?' I thought. 'It isn't like anyone will actually read it.'**

My first inkling that the article had generated rather more attention than I anticipated occurred when I got a spate of interview requests from reporters around the world asking me to comment on the religious dimensions of Apple. Somewhat worryingly, in explaining how they had learned about my 'research', several referenced articles by writers whose names bore no resemblance to the journalist I'd actually talked to. A brief but appalled search of Google followed, along with the dawning realization that the story

*Tim Bell, I'm talking to you.

**Yes, well, I realize how stupid that sounds *now*. I also fully acknowledge that agreeing to do a light-hearted interview in the first place ranks up there with the time I decided to perm my own hair for acts of stupidity with embarrassingly public results.

had been taken up by scores of media outlets and bloggers. Headlines screamed: 'Anthropologist "confirms" Apple is a religion', 'Anthropologists think Apple has become a religion', 'Apple is a modern religion, anthropologist confirms'. It became apparent that, like the game of Chinese Whispers* we used to play at school, the story had become utterly transformed in the retelling. I was no longer someone who'd done something as mundane as watching a couple of YouTube clips. In some articles, I had attended the iPad Mini launch; other more imaginative souls had me conducting long-term fieldwork at Apple. In one account, I'd drawn my 'conclusions' from a survey of Apple fans. Even worse were the subsequent academic critiques, which treated my light-hearted comments as if they reflected a serious, albeit deficient, scholarly study. The ignominy of this fiasco followed me around for years, as these articles were prominently featured on Google's cursed search algorithms—when, that is, they weren't bringing up articles about the actress Kristen Bell.

While this experience made me wary of engaging with a broader audience, especially on topics I can't claim any direct research expertise in, it's long been clear that many of the subjects that intrigue me most are of little interest to my fellow academics—being considered too low-

---

*This is the name (in Australia at least, although I believe it goes by the more politically correct appellation 'Telephone' elsewhere) of a game where a group of kids sit in a circle and one comes up with a sentence and whispers it in the ear of the next kid, who whispers it to the next kid, and so on and so forth until the last child is reached and whispers the sentence—now utterly transformed—back into the ear of the original child. To much general hilarity, an innocuous saying like 'Mary wants a cracker' might become transformed into 'Mary's crackers', then 'Mary's gone around the bend', and finally 'Mary's doing knee bends'. Sometimes things become so distorted that you miraculously end up back where you started. That did not happen here.

brow for scholarly study. The first scholarly paper I ever tried to publish was inspired by the side notes I'd written during my fieldwork rather than my formal dissertation project. Called 'Silent but deadly: Bodily odours and the dissipation of boundaries', I submitted it to a prestigious academic journal, confident that I'd hit on an understudied topic and that the paper would soon become a classic in the field. The reviewers, however, hated it. 'This looks like a graduate school essay cobbled together at the end of the year', one ranted.* The consensus was that this was not serious scholarship and the manuscript was rejected outright. Thoroughly demoralized, I put the paper aside and focused my efforts on 'proper' scholarly publications. However, I continued to write down observations about everyday beliefs and behaviours—my computer was soon full of files with notes and musings on the minutia of daily life. Generally, these pieces were sparked by an incident that annoyed me, embarrassed me, bemused me, or an argument where I felt compelled to prove I was right.**

Many remain unfinished—such as vexed notations about lane etiquette at my local swimming pool, but where my ire soon abated. These observations were often incorporated into undergraduate lectures, and some became the basis of short articles I wrote for newspapers and blogs; others languished on my computer for decades in note form because I wasn't sure what to do with them. The idea of writing a book didn't occur to me until recently. After

---

*Most academics can quote their first review chapter and verse, especially if it was vicious, which they often are, academic peer review basically constituting a form of verbal blood sport. In hindsight, this was one of the more moderate reviews I've received in my career.

**Basically every argument ever. You will soon discover, dear reader, that I don't like to be wrong.†

†It helps, of course, that I almost never am.

the website *Popanth*, where I'd published a few pieces, temporarily shut down, several people contacted me asking for copies of articles. I realized that perhaps there was some appetite for these musings after all. The title of this book, while echoing the name of the first chapter (based, in part, on the most popular article I published on *Popanth*), also alludes to the fact that these cultural patterns are mostly invisible ('silent', as it were), but also 'deadly'—a term I use in its Aboriginal Australian sense to mean 'cool' or 'awesome'.

In case it's not abundantly clear, my focus in what follows is not life's big questions but the little ones. In this book, I'm more interested in toilet paper shortages than the collapse of civilizations, body odours than environmental pollutants, tipping than capitalism, farting than feminism, and swearing than social inequality. There are plenty of books—big, serious books—about these other topics. This book, on the other hand, isn't that big or, it must be said, that serious. However, I hope to show that even little questions—like 'Why do farts evoke laughter and disgust?' and 'Is the aversion to the left hand universal?'—have big answers, illuminating what binds us together as humans and what separates us as creatures of custom and habit.

In total, *Silent but Deadly* consists of thirteen discrete essays on an eclectic array of topics. Although each essay stands alone and the chapters can be dipped into and out of as time and interest demand, I have structured the book so that certain underlying threads are evident if it's read from start to finish. The first five chapters, focusing respectively on farting, body odours, toilet paper, teeth, and washing machines, deal, broadly speaking, with the body and cleanliness—a common thread is how we conceptualize 'dirt'—although this is also a recurring theme throughout the book. The following five chapters, examining animal classifications, our cultural obsession with dogs, stock market terminology, the logic of tipping, and pub drinking rituals, deal broadly with themes of classification and exchange. The final three chapters, which delve into swearing, handedness, and numbers, deal primarily with natural symbols—symbols that straddle the line between nature and culture.

By deciphering the cultural patterns that underlie our everyday quirks, foibles, and habits, I hope to convince you that even the most seemingly mundane behaviours provide us with fascinating insights into what it is to be human, in all our strangeness and pettiness, but also our creativity and ingenuity. So come into my parlour, friend; make yourself comfortable and pull up a chair. For I have many curious things to show you there.

1

Silent but Deadly

Twenty years ago, while I was lecturing at a regional university in Colorado, a colleague had a somewhat odd encounter with a student. This student (let's call him Steve) had approached her about a recent incident, wanting her anthropological opinion on its meaning. As she recounted it to me, while waiting for a class to start, Steve yawned and stretched in his chair and accidentally let out an audible fart—the brunt of which was borne by a classmate sitting directly behind him. Offended by the errant fart, his classmate insisted that Steve apologize. When Steve refused, his irate classmate responded with threats to beat him up. Bewildered at the response his fart engendered, Steve asked my colleague why this natural occurrence was treated with such hostility.

Now to most people (other than Steve, who was a slightly unusual bloke), his fellow student's response to the fart, although extreme, is somewhat understandable.*

---

*I, for one, have occasionally been tempted to violence by the relentless—and blatantly unrepentant—olfactory abuse my husband has subjected me to for decades.

You only need to watch fart prank videos on YouTube to confirm that not everyone takes kindly to strangers unapologetically farting in their vicinity.* In one encounter filmed by the American comedian Jack Vale, a Walmart patron is so incensed by Vale's failure to apologize for seeming to crop-dust** the aisle where his wife is perusing home improvement gadgets from the seat of her mobility scooter that he follows Vale around the store and punches him in the face. 'That was my wife's face,' the indignant shopper proclaims as Vale tries to explain the prank; 'you stood right there and did it constantly!'

The associations of intentional farting with insult abound—from John Cleese's Frenchman in *Monty Python and the Holy Grail* threatening to fart in the 'general direction' of King Arthur and his band of horseless knights to a recent 'fart bullying' lawsuit in which an Australian employee sued his former company $1.8 million for dam-

---

*Notably, these pranksters don't actually fart, but employ hidden fart-sound devices. (Jack Vale's videos seem to effectively be advertisements for his 'pooter' fart-sound device.) I assume this is because of the challenges of farting on demand (not a problem my husband shares), but also because uncontrolled flatulence—which typically precedes a severe bout of diarrhoea—is distinctly less funny than someone pretending to fart.

**'Crop-dusting' is a term used to describe farting while walking through a crowd or group. Legend (well, at least the *The Sun*, a British tabloid) suggests that it was coined by flight attendants to describe their practice of walking down the passenger aisle when the urge to fart comes upon them, thereby inflicting the stench on unsuspecting passengers rather than their colleagues in the galley.† The typical form is stealthy crop-dusting—the idea is to move fast enough so that the source of the smell can't be identified. Obviously, anonymity can only be maintained if the fart has no sound.

†The next time you're on a long-haul flight silently cursing that unknown passenger somewhere in your vicinity who is periodically expelling rank farts, pause to consider whether the smirking flight attendant who just served your drink might instead be the culprit.

ages for workplace bullying. The crux of his case was the behaviour of his supervisor, nicknamed 'Mr Stinky', who would allegedly come into the claimant's office and 'lift his bum and fart' up to six times a day.* Although the claimant lost the case and his subsequent appeal on the grounds that flatulence did not necessarily constitute harassment and bullying, the fact that legal experts debated the meanings of farting in court (twice!) brings us right back to Steve's question.

So why do farts potentially evoke hostility, shame, laughter, and disgust? The interesting thing is that anthropologists have never tried to answer this question. While we haven't generally been afraid to get down and dirty in our subject matter, we apparently draw the line at farts. Are we prepared to take Diane Ackerman's word for it in *A Natural History of the Senses* that 'though ancient and uncontrollably natural, a fart is generally considered to be repellent, discourteous, and even the smell of the devil'? Call it an insatiable curiosity about the human condition, call it a Freudian anal fixation, but I, for one, am not willing to let the matter rest there. So, in the interest of sharing the fruits of my intellectual labours, I present to you some anthropological reflections on farts.

Tellingly, humans are the only primates that react to farts.** Having grilled primatologist colleagues at length

*I suspect this isn't the last we've heard of fart bullying. Employment law firms in the USA have quickly cottoned onto the idea that workplace farting constitutes a form of bullying, with an employment firm in New Hampshire recently advising, 'If you get "wind" of such a workplace bullying case, you should consult a New Hampshire employment law attorney'.

**Based on the number of Quora queries about whether cats and dogs respond to farts, and helpful responses from readers who have farted in their pets' faces,† many dogs do react to farts, but this seems to be largely an artefact of their intriguing smell, rather than stemming from

on this topic, it's clear that our closest relatives are blithely unconcerned by the act—something borne out by footage of chimps and gorillas farting in zoos and the wild. I therefore suspect that our distinctive response to farts is just as central to the story of what it means to be human as our opposable thumbs and capacity to control fire. Yet, no topic more discussed in popular culture has been less discussed by anthropologists—witness Constance Classen, David Howe, and Anthony Synnott's book *Aroma: The Cultural History of Smell*, in which farts are relegated to a single page.

Despite this general dearth, something approaching a grand theory of farting can be found in the German sociologist Norbert Elias's masterpiece *The Civilizing Process*. Writing at the cusp of the Second World War, Elias suggested that radical changes in social standards occurred in Europe between the fourteenth and nineteenth centuries. In particular, there was an expanding threshold of repugnance (i.e., feelings of shame and embarrassment) around natural bodily functions—from eating and farting to sexual intercourse—due to the growing European preoccupation with 'civilized' and 'barbaric' behaviour. This preoccupation with manners and civility developed first in the secular upper classes, who saw their adoption of cutlery and coyness regarding their bodily functions as evidence of their superiority to peasants, but filtered down to the middle and lower classes. Thus, actions that people didn't blink an eye at in the thirteenth century were considered unmannerly by the sixteenth. For example, like his forebears, the sixteenth-century Dutch philosopher

---

any sort of value judgement regarding their owners. As we all know, dogs certainly don't react to their *own* farts.

†This is virtually unavoidable if one has a cat. As more than one Quora respondent pointed out, given cats' penchant for cosy spaces, their face is usually *right there* when the urge to fart comes upon one in bed.

and theologian Desiderius Erasmus believed it unhealthy to repress farts, but counselled children to withdraw, if possible, when the urge to break wind came upon them or, if this improved impossible, to 'replace farts with coughs'.

As the historian Valerie Allen illustrates in *On Farting: Language and Laughter in the Middle Ages*, the association of farts with shame and the dangers posed by misplaced flatulence (as well as its connection with ribald humour) are evident throughout the Middle Ages. Indeed, this seems a particularly rich period for flatologists because, while embarrassing and shameful, farts were not yet so rude as to be stricken entirely from polite conversation. An encounter between Queen Elizabeth I and Edward de Vere, the seventeenth Earl of Oxford, illustrates the point. According to Allen, after accidentally farting while bowing to the Queen, de Vere immediately retired to the Continent for seven years. Upon his eventual return to court, Queen Elizabeth greeted him warmly with, 'My lord, I had forgot the Fartt.'

Of course, if unintentional farts are considered shameful and embarrassing, they can also be *intentionally* deployed to express inverse emotions such as disgust and contempt. It's precisely this meaning that is evoked in *The Papal Belvedere* woodcut featured in one of Martin Luther's heretical pamphlets railing against the Catholic Church, with its depiction of German peasants farting at Pope Paul III (see figure 1). Farts take on similarly seditious qualities two and a half centuries later in a satiric cartoon featuring John Bull—a figure widely employed as a personification of England—farting at a poster of King George III, while the British Prime Minister, William Pitt the Younger, declares it a treasonous act (see figure 2).

Intriguingly, the association of farting with contempt is not an exclusively Western response, suggesting the po-

Figure 1. *The Papal Belvedere* by Lucas Cranach the Elder, 1545

tential limits of Elias's analysis. Frank Muir, in *An Irreverent and Almost Complete Social History of the Bathroom*, cites an early report from the 1600s in which Papua New Guinean witnesses to flatulent Dutch sailors were deeply offended by the farts they were subjected to, holding that a 'shame and contempt' had been done to them. Their Polynesian neighbours on the Marquesan Islands employed intentional farts to similar effect in their own colonial encounters with Europeans. According to the anthropologist Nicholas Thomas, islanders would thrust out their arses and fart at missionaries to communicate precisely what they thought of the Christian message.

One of the few anthropologists to have delved into

Figure 2. *Treason!!!* by Richard Newton, 1798

farting is Edward Westermarck. In *Ritual and Belief in Morocco*, based on fieldwork conducted in Morocco in the first quarter of the twentieth century, Westermarck observed that bodily uncleanness is injurious to *baraka*, an Arabic word meaning 'blessing' or 'holiness'. Thus, sexual congress affects *baraka*, but, at least at the time of his fieldwork, so too did excremental impurity. Farting in a mosque was consequently a dangerous act, serving to impurify the space and displease the spirits within, typically inciting supernatural payback in the form of blindness or invasion by evil influences. Westermarck wrote that areas where the offence had publicly occurred were marked by stones and considered bad luck.

But the meaning of farting seemed to extend well beyond the realm of uncleanliness in terms of the responses it evoked. According to Westermarck, intense disgrace was attached to involuntary public farts, whether emanating from a five-year-old boy or a grown man—the only difference being the severity of their consequences. While the child could expect a beating from his peers, men often made a hasty departure from the village after succumbing to an ill-timed fart, never to be heard of again. Westermarck also suggested, in perhaps overly credulous tones, that 'In Berber tribes I have even heard of cases of suicide committed in consequence of such an act'. However, he observed that the severe social penalties attached to farting were not uniform throughout Morocco—in Fes, for example, farting was considered healthy rather than shameful.

A detailed examination of the meaning of farts is also found in the work of the anthropologists Anthony Seeger and Jon Crocker, who have conducted fieldwork amongst related indigenous groups in Brazil: the Suyá and Bororo, respectively. According to their individual accounts, in both groups, farts are classified under 'rotten smells' and perceived as dangerous and powerful—crucial to avoid where possible. When faced with the olfactory invasion of the fart, both the Suyá and the Bororo respond by spitting; when anyone farts in public, the whole group must go through an elaborate ritual of hacking, spitting, and coughing to expel the polluting odour from their bodies.* For the Suyá, the only exception to the general spitting rule is when the fart emanates from one's parents-in-law. In such situations, Seeger's informants warned, one must

---

*Seeger was the focus of much concern for his own failure to spit in such situations, based on Suyá fears that he would begin to rot internally by failing to eject the dangerous odour from his body.

literally suck it up—taking one's chances 'in the interest of an etiquette of silence and respect'.

Accounts from other cultural contexts also allude to the complex relationship between farting and social status. According to the Taiwanese anthropologist Lily Wen, a member of the Rukai (one of Taiwan's indigenous communities), during the Japanese colonial period, courtship rituals amongst the Rukai occurred under the watchful eye of the girl's family. If the boy farted during the performance of a love ballad—a key component of courting rituals—he had to pay reparations to her family. According to Wen, given that the Rukai had a legume-based diet, this was a not-infrequent occurrence.*

Such fears are somewhat comprehensible to the average Brit, Australian, or North American, as the thought of releasing an audible fart during a speech, presentation, or meeting is enough to make most people (myself included) break into a cold sweat. Silent or virtually soundless farts are certainly the best option in this context, although, if they are accompanied by a strong smell, the conditions must be such that anonymity can be preserved.** Indeed,

---

*The rhyming song *Beans* (as in 'Beans, beans good for the heart; beans, beans make you fart; the more you fart, the better you feel, so eat baked beans for every meal') is not, as you may have assumed, a puerile children's ditty but a public service announcement helpfully presented in couplet form. While endless nutritional studies have highlighted the link between beans and heart health, in 1988 the food scientist Keith Price and his colleagues finally confirmed what we'd all long suspected: legumes do indeed increase flatulence.

**Many of us are aware of 'phantom farters'—people wont to regularly slip out 'silent-but-deadlies' in public situations, causing a frenzy of surreptitious air sniffing and disgusted sideways glances as everybody tries to make it subtly but pointedly clear that they, too, are aware of the offensive odour and it certainly didn't emanate from them! If American employment law firms have their way, this might ultimately become a prosecutable offense.

the alleged desire of the French writer Honoré de Balzac to one day be 'so well known, so popular, so celebrated, so famous, that it would... permit me to break wind in society and society would think it a most natural thing' has the ring of a utopian dream. *Nobody* gets to fart with impunity. However, it's also clear that not all farts are equal—in other words, who the farter is and whom they fart around seem to be critical factors.

Certainly, in a North American context, some public farts appear to be judged less harshly than others, with the farts of the elderly and small children evoking relatively little response.* These differences are especially prominent in Jack Vale's hidden camera footage of his fart pranks with hapless shoppers. When he dresses up as an old man, the responses are markedly more tolerant than when he fake-farts as himself (a youthful-looking man in his forties). In his elderly disguise, shoppers are alternately amused, annoyed, and disgusted by his overt and unrepentant flatulence, but most of them seem prepared to accept that 'old farts' live up to their name. The relaxation of social mores around farting for these two age groups speaks to the ways in which the very young and the very old tend to converge in our perception—both being placed into the category of 'not yet socialized/too old to care'.

However, responses to public farts are crosscut not just by age but by gender.** Notably, none of the fart prank-

---

*Like the Suyá man suffering silently through the emissions of his wife's parents as a sign of respect, upon being confronted with a series of staccato farts produced by an elderly farter, the most appropriate response is to continue the conversation with both parties pretending that nothing out of the ordinary has occurred.

**Private farts are, of course, a different matter. Breaking wind, for better or worse, is a sign of intimacy and familiarity—the higher our degree of comfort with the person, the more likely we are to voluntarily

sters on YouTube are women, and female celebrities often go to extreme lengths to deny culpability for farts.* Indeed, I have seen t-shirts proclaiming 'girls don't fart'. Whether taken as a statement of fact or a plea for anal rectitude, the meaning is clear: 'ladies' are not supposed to fart. This leads women to attempt to become virtually fartless at best and 'silent-but-deadly' farters at worst.** Even a fart in a public toilet booth can be a source of considerable embarrassment for women—leading to elaborate tactics to avoid attribution, from the strategic deployment of Erasmus's advice ('replace farts with coughs') to waiting in the toilet stall until the patrons in the remaining booths have left.

Obviously, farts contain several sensory dimensions that might help explain the hostile reactions they are liable to receive: many of them are accompanied by noise, they are associated with faecal matter, and can be lit to rather startling effect. However, it's unquestionably the odour of farts that is the source of their offensiveness. As Benjamin Franklin once wrote: 'Were it not for the odiously offensive smell accompanying such escapes, polite people would probably be under no more restraint in discharging such wind in company than they are in spitting

---

fart around them. Nevertheless, it is typically the man who farts first in heterosexual relationships—at least, based on informal surveys I have conducted over the years with my undergraduate students.

*Even Whoopi Goldberg, who took her stage name from a whoopee cushion, frequently jokes about farting, and has appeared to fart on air on the show *The View* several times, has felt the need to (ahem) clear the air in several interviews by stating, 'I don't fart on air for real!'

**A co-worker once gave me tips on how you can minimize the danger of being identified as the bearer of a 'silent-but-deadly' fart. The trick, she explained, is to wave your hand frantically behind your arse upon expelling the fart and then jump away from the now ostensibly detached smell—leaving it to linger unmoored from its earthly bearer, just like the demonic fog described in the James Herbert story.

or blowing their noses'. For most of us, the sound of a fart signifies—rightly or wrongly—that a malodourous scent will shortly follow.*

Benjamin Franklin appears to be onto something. The anthropologist Mary Douglas has famously argued that bodily refuse (such as mucous, spittle, blood, and nail clippings) is often tabooed—universally seen as a symbol of power and danger because it traverses the body's boundaries. Extending these ideas, the feminist philosopher Julia Kristeva argues that the matter expelled from the body is 'abject'—it simultaneously revolts and fascinates us because it 'disturbs identity, system, order'. The abject distorts the lines between what is 'me' and what is 'not me' because it escapes one body and attacks the boundaries of others. As the French philosopher Jean-Paul Sartre observed, when we smell another person's body, it's as if we're breathing in the actual person; in his words, 'Once inhaled, the smell is the fusion of the other's body and my own'.

Farts may very well be the ultimate bodily emission. They are likely to be perceived as far more polluting than bodily excretions such as faeces because they are, for all intents and purposes, invisible—we can't actively avoid them. While we can generally side-step faeces, blood, and urine, or complain to the waiter if we find a hair in our soup, little can be done to protect ourselves from the sensory invasion of the fart. According to the anthropologist

---

*To use the language of the semiotician Charles Sanders Peirce (semiotics is the study of signs and symbols), it's an indexical sign, where there is a cause-effect relationship between the signifier and signified. Just as a smoke signifies fire, the sound of a fart signifies the smell of a fart. Much of the 'deadliness' of the silent-but-deadly stems from the fact that it disrupts the usual perceived cause-effect relationship: it is a signified without a signifier (or perhaps more accurately, the signifier and signified have collapsed into each other). Sadly, the semiotics of farting is yet to be explored in depth.

Annick Le Guérer: 'A smell is unavoidable, for it cannot be either voided or avoided through a rejective process like vomiting'. Of course, the Suyá and Bororo Indians make an attempt via spitting and hacking—responses that highlight the invasive capacities of the fart. A parallel effort to stave off invasion is evident in the common tendency to hold one's breath upon stepping into a lift and registering that its previous occupant has left a parting gift. However, in both cases, the attempt is unsuccessful—like death itself, the fart will not be denied entry.

So, the next time you fart, whether it be alone in an elevator, or surreptitiously during a meeting (phantom farters, you know who you are), or when you have just settled into bed and your partner lifts the covers to climb in and is greeted by an unwanted surprise, pause for a moment to contemplate the abject power of the fart. In one quite literally foul swoop, the fart momentarily* destroys our allusions regarding the integrity and autonomy of the human body—our certainty and security regarding the boundaries between what is 'me' and what is 'not me'—and reveals both its fragility and vulnerability.

---

*Actually, for as much as ten minutes in the case of some particularly pungent farts. This often leads to a heated debate (in my household, at least) about what will remove the smell most quickly: a frenetic bout of sheet flapping or leaving the smell trapped underneath the covers until it eventually dies—like a wounded animal that has crawled into a small, dark place to wait out its final hours.

2

Pits of Despair

When I lived in Vancouver, I regularly took a bus route to work that attracted some rather eccentric characters. On one occasion, I entered the bus during the afternoon rush hour and noticed an empty seat next to an old, dishevelled-looking woman wearing a hospital gown. Thrilled to find a seat, I registered as I sat down next to her that she reeked of booze, a factor that I assumed explained the empty space—that is until she spoke.

I had just put my bag on my lap when she turned around and glared at me. 'God, you stink,' she exclaimed loudly. Startled and assuming I'd misheard, I stammered, 'Excuse me?' She said it again, but slowly this time, in case I was deaf. 'God, you STINK. You smell like you haven't had a shower for a WEEK!' Embarrassed that everyone on the bus could hear her, and indignant that someone who smelled like she'd bathed in a vat of beer was commenting on my own body odour, I figured she was drunk—and confused about whose odour she was smelling to boot—and decided to ignore her. But she'd only just begun. 'You stink, you smell, stinky poo, stinky poo,' she repeated over and over in a high-pitched sing-song voice. After about thirty seconds of this, and with everyone else on the bus studiously ignoring us, I hastily vacated the seat.

At the next bus stop, I watched another hapless woman get on, her face lighting up as she spotted the vacant space next to the old woman. As she hurried to sit down, I thought perhaps I should warn her that the seat was a trap, waiting to snare unsuspecting passengers, but I couldn't be sure that she was about to be subjected to a repeat of the treatment I'd just received. Having clearly been around this block a few times now, everyone else within hearing distance waited with bated breath as the woman sat down. Sure enough, the old woman didn't disappoint. Looking her new seat mate up and down, she loudly announced, 'God, you're fat. You're so fat you must be a size sixteen. You're a fatty! Fatty, fatty, fatty.' 'Don't take it personally,' I reassured the woman as she quickly vacated the seat. 'She told me I smelled.'

Still, the incident left me feeling paranoid. If the old lady had also attacked the other woman's smell, I could have chalked it up to booze and insanity,* but it felt like she'd tailored her insults to each of us. The woman was slightly plump, so perhaps I did smell, I reasoned as I walked home. Worried that the old lady on the bus was just stating a truth that my colleagues had been too polite to share, I took my coat to the dry cleaner the following day and doubled up on deodorant; I no longer trusted my nose.

This incident speaks to our peculiar obsession with bodily odour. Although we often treat our sense of smell as less significant than our other senses, encounters such as this reveal its powerful role in human interaction. As the

---

*If she was crazy, she was crazy like a fox, because I'm pretty sure she just wanted the seat to herself to sleep off her hangover.

evolutionary biologist Michael Stoddart observes in *The Scented Ape*, 'If the human nose is vestigial, with powers only a fraction of what they were in our distant ancestry, why are humans so concerned about odours?' And why are body odours such an intense preoccupation?

Unlike farts, most odours are excreted by the body in a continuous rather than discrete fashion. This allows them to recede into the background in a way impossible for the fart—which, you may recall, is typically signified by a *sound* as much as a *smell* and has a fleeting presence. While our skin and hair emanate odours, these smells are most potent at the body's orifices (mouth, anus, genitals) and those sites where our sweat glands are concentrated, such as the armpits and groin. These smells may intensify due to various activities—eating, exercising, and sexual intercourse have this effect—but a key attribute of bodily odours is that they are continuously present. All of us have a unique odour signature that is as much a part of our identity as our sex and our skin colour, albeit less consciously registered.

Stoddart discusses the significance of this odour signature for recognition, both in humans and other mammals. He argues that while humans' capacity to distinguish people based on their odour is inferior to other primates, this sense is better developed than we think. Thus, studies have shown that breastfed babies quickly learn to recognize their mother's scent, and mothers likewise can correctly identify their infants by odour. Parents can distinguish which of their children has worn a particular shirt by smell alone, and siblings can discriminate each other's odours in the same fashion. Kin also have similar odour signatures—Stoddart observes that dogs can track down an identical twin after being exposed to the scent of their sibling.

Amplifying these biological similarities in odour signatures amongst kin is the role played by diet, which also affects body odour. As the cultural historian Constance Classen notes, this means that bodily odours often differ from group to group and culture to culture. However, because we're so accustomed to our own personal and group odours, we only notice the odours of others.*

An example of this phenomenon can be found in the anthropologist Edmund Carpenter's book *Eskimo Realities*, in which he recounts a conversation with Kowanerk, an Inuit woman of his acquaintance. In the context of discussing Inuit sensibilities around politeness and concerns not to offend, he writes,

> One day when Kowanerk and I were alone, she looked up from the boot she was mending to ask, without preamble, 'Do we smell?'
> 'Yes.'
> 'Does the odor offend you?'
> 'Yes.'
> She sewed in silence for a while, then said, 'You smell and it's offensive to us. We wondered if we smelled and if it offended you.'

This encounter illustrates not only cultural differences in body odour but cultural differences in assessments of what is malodourous. In *Aroma: The Cultural History of Smell*, Constance Classen, David Howes, and Anthony Synnott in-

---

*The same is true of accents, which we tend to think that only other people have. I distinctly remember the first time I consciously registered the nature of an Australian accent. I was ten and my family and I were at a US airport waiting for our flight back to Australia, having lived overseas for a year. After months of hearing nothing but rounded vowels and exaggerated 'r's (beyond the accents of my family, which remained invisible to me), my siblings and I could suddenly *hear* the nasal undertones and flat vowels in the accents of the Australians gathered at the airport and were shocked (unpleasantly, it must be said) that this is how we sounded to others.

sist that 'the categories of the fragrant and the foul are not given in nature, but rather come from culture. There are no natural likes or dislikes in matters olfactory'. I suspect this is an overstatement—skunks appear to have evolved the ability to emit noxious odours precisely because the smell is universally abhorred amongst predators (including humans). There may also be some smells, such as the stench of death, which humans instinctively fear for very sound evolutionary reasons—namely, it steers them clear of diseased and contaminated corpses. Most people also find the distinctive 'rotten egg' smell of hydrogen sulphide unpleasant, which likewise performs a useful biological function, given that high levels of exposure lead to respiratory failure. But there is clearly more at work in our reception of odour than biology and evolution. Therefore, while the categories of the foul and the fragrant might not be entirely culturally determined, they do seem to be strongly culturally mediated—especially when it comes to bodily odours. The problem is that our reaction seems natural because of the immediacy of the physical response odours evoke. To quote Diane Ackerman in *A Natural History of the Senses*, 'Unlike other senses, smell needs no interpreter. The effect is immediate and undiluted by language, thought, or translation'.

In light of our physiological response to those who smell different from ourselves, it's little surprise that the word 'stinking' comes up so frequently in racial invective.*

---

*Of course, it's not just employed in racial invective, but makes a handy insult regardless of the context—as I discovered on the bus in Vancouver. I recall being entertained in a working-class Irish pub by the conversation of two truck drivers sitting at the next table, who were loudly regaling each other with details of recent encounters with 'smelly fookin' coonts', an expression they flung around with abandon throughout the conversation. I will have much more to say about in-

Indeed, Classen argues that body odour often serves as a scapegoat for broader antipathies towards the other, with members of one group or culture attributing an exaggeratedly offensive odour to those they feel general animosity towards. These tendencies are far from new—Classen notes that the most common insult used by the ancient Incans for their Collasuyu neighbours was 'stinking' (*aznay*). Similarly, anti-Semitism in Europe in the Middle Ages was often accompanied by accounts of the 'stench' of the Jews, and British and French colonizers in Africa frequently complained about 'stinking' natives. Europeans were so convinced of their superior smell that they were often surprised to learn that their own scent was considered foul by those they colonized. For example, according to Classen, the Serer Ndut of Senegal characterized Europeans as smelling like urine, with mothers warning children who disliked bathing to be careful lest they smell urinous like white people.

Notably, aspersions about a group's perceived bodily odour have frequently been cast on the basis of class as well as culture. George Orwell captured this sentiment in *The Road to Wigan Pier* in his observation, 'The real secret of class distinctions in the West can be summed up in four frightful words: The lower classes smell'. According to Orwell, class differences in odour were used to naturalize perceptions of the inferiority of the working class. Likewise, the cultural historian Alain Corbin has discussed at length how the French upper class came to justify their elevated social position on the basis of their superior smell. As the anthropologist Annick Le Guérer observes, the invention of domestic plumbing played a critical role in stoking class hatred because of the ways it reinforced smell-based social

sults in 'You Can't Say "C*nt" in Canada'.

divisions.

The moral connotations of body odour are also evident in the growing tendency of vegetarians and vegans to flaunt their superior smell to meat-eaters. Indeed, this seems to be one of the few contexts where commenting on such differences is socially acceptable. These declarations trace back to a small Czech study that found that women rated the body odour of male subjects as more attractive after the men abstained from meat for two weeks. However, a later Australian study found precisely the opposite: meat-eaters were thought to have the most pleasant odour.*

Assertions about the odoriferous inferiority of meat-eaters speak to the ways in which differences in odour become value-laden and politicized—an idea taken to its logical conclusion in 'The Chromium Fence', a short story by the American sci-fi writer Philip K. Dick. In the story, the Purists, who voluntarily remove their sweat glands, submit to breath control, have artificial waste excretion tubes installed, whiten their teeth,** and restore their hair, are

---

*It's entirely plausible that Czech and Australian women might differ in which male body odours they find attractive—a possibility that both sets of researchers fail to consider. This is primarily because of the obsession amongst evolutionary psychologists with the search for human pheromones: chemicals released by some animals that change the behaviour of other animals, especially in mating. Since the discovery of pheromones in the 1950s, countless men and women have been subjected to sweat samples from members of the opposite sex in the name of science. However, because adult humans don't have a functioning vomeronasal organ, solid evidence on the role of pheromones in human sexual attraction is notably lacking. Still, plenty of people are willing to pay good money for perfumes claiming to produce a frenzy of sexual desire in the opposite sex—as vividly illustrated by ladies' man Brian Fantana's 'Sex Panther' perfume in the movie *Anchorman* ('it's illegal in nine countries'), although his cologne ends up provoking more of a gag reflex than a shag reflex.

**I shall have much more to say about this topic in 'Going to the

at war with the Naturalists over their different ideological views. 'You Naturalists have nothing to offer the future,' a Purist rants; 'You're anti-civilization.'

As Dick's story suggests, this growing concern to eradicate natural body odour is clearly part of the broader cultural shifts that Norbert Elias mapped in *The Civilizing Process*, as Europeans' threshold of repugnance expanded around bodily functions and emanations due to their growing preoccupation with 'civilized' and 'barbaric' behaviour. Indeed, Sigmund Freud made an explicit connection between civilization and soap in *Civilization and its Discontents*, noting, 'we are not surprised by the idea of setting up the use of soap as an actual yardstick of civilization'. However, this isn't to suggest that only Europeans are concerned with bodily odour. Humans have long used perfumes, along with techniques such as fumigation, to mask and enhance the body's natural odours. Moreover, most cultures seem to distinguish between foul- and pleasant-smelling odours—the anthropologist Claude Lévi-Strauss argued that this is a universal hallmark of human thought. Annick Le Guérer has discussed at length the widespread cross-cultural view of unpleasant smells as a source of disease and death, with pleasant smells seen to disinfect and cure—ideas epitomized in the view that disease resulted from miasma, or 'bad air', which dominated until the emergence of germ theory. But what odours generally, and bodily odours in particular, become marked is culturally and historically variable.

When I was doing fieldwork in Korea in the late 1990s and early 2000s, body odours regarded as 'smelly' (*naem-sae**) emanated primarily from the mouth and feet. The

---

Dentist Bites'.

*Like its English counterpart, the term *naemsae* is ostensibly neutral

emphasis on the latter may relate to the fact that people remove their shoes in indoor spaces, and stinky feet are flagrantly (or, rather, fragrantly) obvious. The former likely stems from the garlic and fermented cabbage-laden nature of Korean cuisine, which led the Japanese to complain about their 'stinking' neighbours—I was told that 'stinks of garlic' used to be a common insult for Koreans. A variety of implements are available in Korea for reducing bad breath, including ones uncommon in Western countries, such as tongue cleaners. One advertisement for Kobiz tongue cleaners plastered all over the Seoul subway in 2002 warned, 'Bad breath affects 85% of the population'. While the occasional ad for under-arm deodorant also made an appearance, no one I knew wore it, and deodorant was almost impossible to purchase in the country—although I don't recall noticing 'BO', even at the height of summer. This may relate to the fact that most Koreans carry a variant on the gene associated with axillary odour; indeed, deodorant companies have not been successful in persuading Koreans that they need to purchase the product, despite their best efforts.*

in Korean—there are specific terms for pleasant and unpleasant smells. But to be told 'you smell' or 'it smells' is rarely a compliment in either language. This comes across clearly in the scene in the Korean movie *Parasite* where the wealthy couple are discussing Mr Kim's smell while he hides under the couch. The emphasis throughout the film on the smell of the Kim family highlights the class dimension of odour I've already discussed.

*The same is true in China. According to a *New York Times* article by Owen Guo, Unilever spent a fortune marketing Rexona to Chinese consumers in the lead up to the Beijing Olympics. The campaign was a complete failure. This was partly attributed to biological differences in sweat patterns between Chinese and Americans, but also to the cultural meanings of sweat, which has more positive associations in China. The meanings of sweat in other parts of North Asia are similar—the Japanese sports drink Pocari Sweat is hugely popular in Korea; it's difficult

In contrast, observers have frequently noted the heightened self-consciousness of Americans regarding body odours of all kinds. According to the anthropologist Marybeth MacPhee, American ideas regarding body odour diverged from European practices of personal hygiene in the twentieth century, especially the intensity of the conviction that natural body odours were offensive. MacPhee suggests that this view was self-perpetuating: attempts to eradicate natural bodily odour stimulate a heightened sensitivity to it in a sort of perpetual disgust spiral. As she notes: 'as Americans, we both bathe because we smell and smell because we bathe'.* Indeed, it's difficult to think of a bodily odour Americans *haven't* targeted, from bad breath and BO to stinky vaginas and pungent testicles—the latter being the province of Chassis, a men's personal care product line providing 'Man Care for Down There'. According to the organic chemists John Labows and George Preti, by the 1990s, Americans were spending over a billion dollars annually on products to control their natural aroma—presumably, that figure is much higher now. While the attempt to ruthlessly repress our natural bodily odours has spread internationally, the American arsenal includes

to imagine it performing well in a Western market without a name change, given the image it conjures of someone knocking back a bottle of sweat.

*In other words, if nobody bathed, effectively nobody would smell, because we wouldn't be able to smell ourselves or others. Although cultural historians assure us that if we travelled back to previous centuries, the first thing that would hit us would be the stench, Europeans weren't as sanguine regarding natural bodily odours as we might imagine, although efforts to eradicate them have markedly intensified over the past century. For example, in the English poet Robert Herrick's exceedingly literally named 1648 poem, 'Upon a free Maid, with a foule breath', he writes 'You say you'l kiss me, and I thanke you for it: / But stinking breath, I do as hell abhorre it.'

practices uncommon elsewhere, such as vaginal douching—a procedure I was entirely unfamiliar with before living in the US, when I saw my first Summer's Eve commercial on television.*

The advertising industry has clearly played a vital role in this exquisite American sensitivity to body odour. 'Every orifice in the body has been taken over by commercial interests,' the historian James Twitchell declared in his documentary *Sell and Spin: The History of Advertising.*** Since the first quarter of the twentieth century, Americans have been bombarded with advertisements for products which attempt to annihilate their natural aromas. Listerine mouthwash 'kills germs that cause bad breath', deodorants promise to provide 'antibacterial odour protection', Colgate toothpaste guarantees 'long lasting fresh breath protection', and Kotex Light Days sanitary pads claim to be 'odour absorbing'.

A key element of advertisers' success in marketing deodorizers is the claim that we're probably unaware of our offensive smell. Body odours, the public is warned, can wreck our romantic relationships, undermine our chances of promotion, alienate our friends, and effectively ruin

---

*The ad featured a woman in a white dress smiling delightedly as she sits on a porch swing,† while a saccharine voiceover sings, 'I'm dreaming of summer, cool breezes, fresh air. When I want that feeling, Summer's Eve takes me there.' For the record, the standard American insult 'douchebag' is utterly meaningless for foreigners until they've seen a Summer's Eve commercial, and then it finally makes sense.

†Although it's not clear if she is smiling because she periodically catches a whiff of her delightfully scented vagina, or with anticipation at the prospect of this imminent state of affairs.

**In 'The Chromium Fence', Philip K. Dick places the blame for the Purist ideology squarely on the advertising industry, with a character noting, 'The industrialists hammered away at the people to buy and consume.'

Figure 3. Listerine mouthwash advertisement, 1928

our lives, primarily because we are oblivious to their presence. This has been a constant thread in advertising since Listerine popularized the term 'halitosis' in the 1920s, having plucked it from an obscure medical journal. 'Halitosis doesn't announce itself. You are seldom aware you have it', counselled a Listerine ad from the period (see figure 3). This theme also runs through advertisements for vaginal douching products. Zonite ads from the 1950s frequently featured distressed-looking women and ominous warnings that anyone who neglected her feminine hygiene was in danger of emanating an offensive odour 'even greater than bad breath or body odor—an odor she herself may not detect but is so apparent to people around her'. Based on the success of Febreze's 'nose blind' campaign, which saw sales of their odour-eliminating spray double in just two months, stoking paranoia remains an effective sales strategy.

That advertisers were able to convince consumers that they needed products to deal with a problem they couldn't personally sense or verify is probably a testament to their prowess. But it's also a testament to the extraordinary power of body odour itself. We judge others, and they judge us in turn, on its basis. From class and culture to civility itself, smell plays a subtle but substantial role in our conceptions of difference. As Le Guérer observes, the contemporary silence surrounding smell therefore reveals the very opposite of indifference to it. Indeed, what made my encounter with the old lady on the bus so unusual wasn't that we noticed each other's smell—I was busily, if silently, judging her stench as soon as I sat down—but that she *commented* on it.

Still, perhaps we are finally reaching the limits of efforts to deodorize the body—at least, based on the rising number of people suffering from chemical sensitivities to perfume and other artificial fragrances. Mary MacPhee treats this as a sign that Americans will once again 'become reacquainted with the subtle changes in the smell of the body due to such things as illness or emotional state', embracing the richer olfactory lives of our forebears. But so far, the rejection of artificial scents doesn't seem to have lessened the distaste for natural ones. Nor does 'The Chromium Fence' give us cause for optimism—after all, the Purists won in the end.*

---

*Given that 'The Chromium Fence' was originally published in 1955, if you feel like I've ruined the ending then I guess you'll be shocked to learn that the food source in the 1973 Charlton Heston vehicle *Soylent Green* is human flesh and Darth Vader is Luke's father.

3

For the Love of Toilet Paper

I was in Australia visiting my parents when Covid went global. Within a week, perceptions of Covid shifted radically in the country, but the first sign that things were seriously amiss was the run on toilet paper. In a clip that quickly went viral, three women got into a brawl* at a Sydney supermarket as a middle-aged woman and her adult daughter placed the entirety of the toilet paper stock in their trolley, to the strong objections of another shopper. 'It's not the Thunderdome; it's not Mad Max. We don't need to do that!' a bewildered policeman declared in the aftermath, which resulted in two arrests.

We watched the news that night in disbelief before I turned to my mum and said, 'We should probably pick up an extra pack of toilet paper tomorrow.' The next day, we went to a local supermarket, but the shelves were already bare of toilet paper. It was the same story at the next place. We pulled into a petrol station on the off chance

---

*I mean brawl in a quite literal sense. This wasn't just the exchange of angry words and a bit of argy-bargy—the footage shows the mother and daughter tag-teaming the other woman with the finesse of professional WWF wrestlers.

that it hadn't yet been pillaged and managed to claim a lone four-roll pack. 'That's the last of the dunny paper,' the attendant declared, shaking her head in disbelief. 'We've been completely wiped out.' We chatted for a few minutes about the general craziness before returning to the car. As we were leaving, a man had just finished pumping petrol and went inside to pay. 'Remember to check if they've got any toilet paper!', a woman in the car called to him as he walked to the shop. 'Thank God we got there first,' I thought as we speedily drove off.

Although the extreme lengths Aussies were prepared to go to obtain toilet paper were the focus of much global amusement, Australia was merely the most visible early manifestation of what's been termed the 'Great Toilet Paper Panic of 2020', which followed a similar pattern in countries such as Hong Kong, Japan, the USA, Canada, and the UK. One clip, filmed by an employee of a Canadian Costco, shows a horde of customers armed with jumbo trolleys descending on the toilet paper aisle. Another, filmed by a customer at a British supermarket, shows people scrambling to grab giant-size toilet paper packs. The guy filming can be heard saying over and over in amazement, 'Look at them all. Look at this! Toilet paper! Wow! Look, look, look at this!' He stops commentating long enough to ask someone off-camera, 'You get one for me? Grab one for me,' before returning to the litany of disbelief.

Commentators were quick to explain panic buying in terms of the psychological attributes of the stockpilers. For example, a study by the political scientist Lisa Garbe and her colleagues concluded that people who felt more personally threatened by Covid were more likely to hoard toilet paper. The standard media narrative also highlighted the irrationality of panic buying—'We are all irrational panic shoppers' declared the title of an article in *The New Yorker* by Helen Rosner. According to Rosner, Covid had turned us all into *hamsterkäufe*: a German word meaning 'to hoard like a nervous, bulging-cheeked hamster'.* In her words, 'fear is contagious: when we see people go out of their way to protect themselves from disaster, no matter how unlikely, we don't want to be the only ones left undefended'.

Despite all the talk of irrational consumers, as the economist Alfredo Paloyo notes, far from being a stupid or senseless strategy, stockpiling toilet paper is an entirely logical response in a situation where market equilibrium has been disrupted. In his words, 'if others panic buy, the optimal strategy for you is to do the same, otherwise you'll be left without toilet paper'. As he notes, the fear had a basis in reality as many people witnessed empty shelves. Indeed, if there's a true culprit in the Great Toilet Paper Panic of 2020, it's probably the media. Like me, I bet many people saw the footage of fights and empty supermarket shelves and thought, 'I'd better get an extra pack, just to be on the safe side.' Combined with the rise of just-in-time manufacturing and distribution, the major (and well-publicized) transformation in the purchasing habits of a few, and the incremental changes in the purchasing habits of the rest, were enough to spark an actual shortage.

Of course, toilet paper wasn't the only supermarket staple that became the focus of panic buying, but it was the item that caused the greatest confusion. Commenta-

---

*Some years ago, Douglas Adams and John Lloyd came out with several dictionaries of words that didn't exist in English, but should. Titled *The Meaning of Liff* and *The Deeper Meaning of Liff*, entries included terms such as 'bickerstaffe' ('the person in an office that everyone whinges about in the pub'), 'flunary' ('the safe place you put something and forget where it was'), and 'alcoy' ('wanting to be bullied into having another drink'). However, it's clear that all we really need to do is to learn German, because you can guarantee that any extremely specific action or emotion worthy of its own name already has one in German.

tors frequently expressed surprise that toilet paper was the focus of stockpiling, in addition to foodstuffs and items like hand sanitizer.* To quote a columnist in *Psychology Today*, 'My first thought was that diarrhoea must be a symptom of Coronavirus'. Typically, this declared bewilderment was accompanied by the claim that few pundits could have predicted the run on toilet paper. However, the Great Toilet Paper Panic of 2020 was preceded by several smaller runs on the product, which sheds a rather different complexion on the factors that led to the most recent shortage.

In *Waste: Consuming Postwar Japan*, the historian Eiko Murko Siniawer discusses the Japanese toilet paper shortage of 1973. According to Siniawer, no one is sure how the toilet paper panic started, although it began in Osaka and rumour played a critical role. The turning point seems to have been a television broadcast calling for consumers to use toilet paper rationally and a newspaper story about toilet paper disappearing from shelves. The very next day, hundreds of housewives began to swamp supermarkets to secure a few rolls, and 'mass media coverage helped turn the hoarding into a national story'. From there, the panic buying spread rapidly from Osaka to Tokyo. The government attempted to assuage people's concerns, and the Ministry of International Trade and Industry repeatedly assured everyone that there was plenty of toilet paper to

---

*One journalist went so far as to label it a 'non-essential' item—a statement of such stupendous ignorance, it can only have come from someone who has never been caught out at that crucial moment. This was a common problem when I was growing up because no one could be bothered to replace the empty roll. For some reason, I was often caught short when family members were not in calling distance (or, I strongly suspect, ignoring the pleas emanating from the loo), leading to the moment of desperation where I would turn to the roll itself. You quickly learn that an unfurled toilet roll is *tiny* and that there's no way you're getting out of this without shit on your hands.

go around. Still, shelves were soon bare in supermarkets across the two regions.

Interestingly, the media coverage of the Japanese toilet paper crisis seems to have partially precipitated the run on toilet paper in the USA the following year. According to an article published by Andrew Malcolm in the *New York Times* in 1974, fears seem to have stemmed from a combination of newspaper reportage about the toilet paper panic in Japan, along with a press release from the federal government's National Buying Center about a potential forthcoming shortage in the government's supplies due to contractor issues. However, the turning point was Johnny Carson's joke* on *The Tonight Show* about the news coverage of the shortage. The following day, toilet paper sales increased markedly, culminating in a nationwide shortage. In what should now be a familiar scenario, officers from Scott Paper Company urged calm, saying there was no shortage if people bought normally.** However, according to Malcolm, 'Some consumers may have believed those remarks—until they saw other shoppers wheeling cases of toilet tissue from some stores or signs rationing each buyer to two rolls each'.

These prior shortages suggest that the toilet paper panic of 2020 was less about Covid and more about toilet paper itself. As the anthropologist Grant Jun Otsuki notes,

---

*Johnny Carson's inadvertent influence on the nationwide toilet paper shortage led to a subsequent apology on his show, where he noted, 'I don't want to be remembered as the man who created a false toilet paper scare.' Of course, he's now remembered as the person whose catchphrase inspired Jack Nicholson's psychotic axe-wielder in the movie *The Shining*, which I'm not sure is better.

**Apparently, at least one Chicago store started advertising that there was no shortage of record players in the hopes that this strategy might have cross-product success. But it turns out that record players aren't considered a household staple, even in the Home of the Blues.

toilet paper is what anthropologists term a 'key symbol'. For Siniawer, writing about Japan's run on toilet paper in the 1970s, it had become a cultural symbol of 'cleanliness, comfort, and convenience'. These meanings, Otsuki suggests, are now pan-cultural—at least, if the toilet paper shortage of 2020 is anything to go by.

The cultural studies scholar Jon Stratton goes even further, arguing that toilet paper is an expression of Western civilization. However, as Stratton acknowledges, for a product that has become so integral to life in many Western countries, its introduction is surprisingly recent. For much of history, humans have used an assortment of implements for wiping our arses—although, as Richard Smyth observes in *Bum Fodder: An Absorbing History of Toilet Paper*, the history of 'wipe-breech' is difficult to piece together. He attributes this to the fact that wipers have 'preferred not to dwell on the act of bum-wiping', but it's also because the makeshift nature of implements, along with their ephemeral qualities, means that they have rarely found their way into the archaeological record.

The primary exception is the Roman sponge brush (known as a *xylospongion* or *tersorium*), although the archaeologist Stephen Nash notes that the Romans also used abrasive ceramic discs called *pessoi*. If that sounds painful, consider the pebbles mentioned in *The Book of Purification* (*Kitab Al-Taharah*) by the ninth-century Muslim scholar ibn al-Hajjaj, or the corn cobs immortalized by the Midwestern American writer James Whitcomb Riley. In his nineteenth-century poem 'The Passing of the Backhouse', he writes, 'The torture of the icy seat would make a Spartan sob / For needs must scrape the gooseflesh with a lacerating cob.' Somewhat less wince-inducing are the pamphlets and catalogues that were a staple of outhouses in Western countries; according to Smyth, Sears & Roebuck catalogues were much prized in the USA for this purpose. However, any disposable paper might end up as toilet fodder—my mother tells stories of the *Vogue* dressmaking patterns that adorned her grandmother's outdoor dunny in Australia. Indeed, it has long been a concern amongst those of a literary bent that their artistic efforts might be deemed disposable enough to merit arse-wiping.*

According to Smyth's *Bum Fodder* and Dave Praeger's book *Poop Culture: How America is Shaped by Its Grossest National Product*, the first commercial toilet paper was developed by the New York entrepreneur Joseph Gayetty in 1857. Advertised as 'the greatest necessity of the age' (see figure 4), it was impregnated with aloe and marketed as a remedy for haemorrhoids. Although Gayetty was excoriated by the medical establishment for quackery, the medicated toilet paper caught on. Pretty soon, other companies followed suit, and a host of familiar names quickly dominated the market, including the Scott Company, the first corporation to manufacture toilet paper on a roll. By 1913, Scott's annual sales were in excess of a million dollars, and it had become abundantly clear that there was serious money to be made in cosseting bottoms. Yet, since the invention of perforated paper, modern toilet paper has changed relatively little from these early prototypes. Rolls today don't look that different from what they might have a hundred

---

*This is illustrated in the cautionary preface to Robert Herrick's 1648 book of poetry *The Hesperides and Noble Numbers*, which warns: 'Who with thy leaves shall wipe (at need) / The place, where swelling Piles do breed: / May every ill, that bites, or smarts, / Perplex him in his hinder parts.' According to Smyth, accusations of 'bum-fodder' have long been employed by writers, artists, and composers wanting to express their contempt for lesser works (typically those of rivals and critics). Jonathan Swift was particularly creative in his use of the insult.

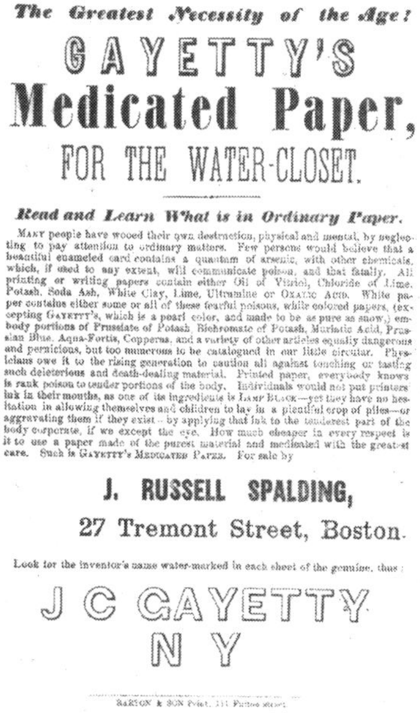

The Greatest Necessity of the Age!

GAYETTY'S

Medicated Paper,

FOR THE WATER-CLOSET.

Read and Learn What is in Ordinary Paper.

MANY people have wooed their own destruction, physical and mental, by neglecting to pay attention to ordinary matters. Few persons would believe that a beautiful enameled card contains a quantum of arsenic, with other chemicals, which, if used to any extent, will communicate poison, and that fatally. All printing or writing papers contain either Oil of Vitriol, Chloride of Lime, Potash, Soda Ash, White Clay, Lime, Ultramine or OXALIC ACID. White paper contains either some or all of these fearful poisons, while colored papers, (excepting GAYETTY'S, which is a pearl color, and made to be as pure as snow,) embody portions of Prussiate of Potash, Bichromate of Potash, Muriatic Acid, Prussian Blue, Aqua-Fortis, Copperas, and a variety of other articles equally dangerous and pernicious, but too numerous to be catalogued in our little circular. Physicians owe it to the rising generation to caution all against touching or tasting such deleterious and death-dealing material. Printed paper, everybody knows is rank poison to tender portions of the body. Individuals would not put printers ink in their mouths, as one of its ingredients is LAMP BLACK—yet they have no hesitation in allowing themselves and children to lay in a plentiful crop of piles—or aggravating them if they exist—by applying that ink to the tenderest part of the body corporate, if we except the eye. How much cheaper in every respect is it to use a paper made of the purest material and medicated with the greatest care. Such is GAYETTY'S MEDICATED PAPER. For sale by

J. RUSSELL SPALDING,

27 Tremont Street, Boston.

Look for the inventor's name water-marked in each sheet of the genuine, thus:

J C GAYETTY
N Y

Figure 4. Advertisement for Gayetty's medicated paper, 1859

years ago, beyond the fact that they're plusher and whiter.*

This isn't to suggest that you *can't* buy coloured toilet paper—there's a whole world of novelty papers out there, from leopard print to bog roll that glows in the dark.** But most of us prefer our toilet paper white. Thus, while

*The primary exception is the bulk toilet paper ubiquitous in office buildings, which has the strength of soggy tissue, the texture of sandpaper, and the colour of used teabags. This, I assume, is both to reduce cost and dissuade potential thieves, although it hasn't proved a very successful deterrent, based on the number of people (myself included) who have flogged toilet paper from their workplace at some point in their lives.

**Although Smyth suggests this one is perhaps best avoided as the coating can rub off the toilet paper, leading to an anus that glows in the dark.

there have been periodic flirtations with pastel shades and subtle floral motifs, manufacturers always revert to white because that's what sells.

At first glance, the colour of toilet paper might seem to be based purely on practical and medical considerations. After all, white enables people to inspect the contents of the tissue to ensure the wiping process is complete. But as Quora attests, many people dispose of used toilet paper without looking at it. I know it's crazy, but not everyone is interested in the answer to questions such as 'How long does it take for corn to pass through one's system?' (Two days) and 'Does beetroot really make it look like you're bleeding internally?' (Why, yes, it does, so don't panic the day after eating it.) Instead, the whiteness of toilet paper is a giveaway that its purpose is symbolic as well as practical. As David Inglis notes in *A Sociological History of Excretory Experience*, the hue of toilet paper derives more from aesthetic and moral criteria than medical stipulations. This is because faeces are what the anthropologist Mary Douglas terms 'dirt'.

In *Purity and Danger*, Douglas argues that contemporary notions of cleanliness are not merely the result of scientific knowledge about the relationship between dirt and disease; moral and aesthetic concerns are equally central. Dirt, according to Douglas, is 'matter out of place', so what is 'dirty' offends not just (or even primarily) medical imperatives but moral ones as well. As I discussed in 'Silent but Deadly', bodily emissions are the ultimate matter out of place. Moreover, such emissions became especially charged in a Western context because of the growing European preoccupation with 'civilized' and 'barbaric' behaviour that Norbert Elias documented in *The Civilizing Process*.

Over the last five centuries, there has been a marked

intensification of feelings of shame and embarrassment around our natural bodily functions. This is why the Romans, armed with their *xylospongion*, had no problem defecating in public, while the Victorians hid the damning evidence in water closets away from public view. As Inglis notes, Western notions of civility were based on the lie that we could rid ourselves of natural bodily processes.* Of course, our bodies repeatedly fail us on this front, which has produced a resultant 'oscillation between self-assurance that one's own body is clean, and despair that it yet produces filth'. According to Inglis, water closets and toilet paper are the way we manage the anxiety induced by the gap between the ideal and reality because they allow us to minimize physical and symbolic contact with our bodily excretions.

The colour white contributes to the lie of the clean, pure body, because of its broader symbolic associations, especially in Christianity, where the colour frequently represents purity, holiness, and redemption. The symbolic efficacy of white in this context may also relate to the colour symbolism discussed by the anthropologist Victor Turner. Based on his fieldwork amongst the Ndembu (located in present-day Zambia), Turner observed that white, red, and black featured prominently in Ndembu rites of passage, with white signifying goodness, health, and purity; black signifying badness, disease, and impurity; and red expressing power and danger. Turner speculated that this related to the biological associations of these colours: white with semen and breast milk, red with blood, and black with excreta. Viewed in this light, white is more symbolically appropriate for the business of arse-wiping than black or red

---

*As a child, I was absolutely convinced that the Queen did not defecate. I recall being extremely shocked to learn otherwise.

because it represents the opposite of faeces. In effect, an arse wiped with white paper *feels* cleaner than one wiped with any other colour.

This is primarily why novelty patterned and coloured toilet papers have never caught on.* It's also why treatises on the benefits of washing over wiping tend to fall on deaf Anglophone ears. For example, in Indi Samarajiva's *Medium* article titled 'White people, you need to wash your butts', he writes: 'You can't just wipe it until the paper looks clean.** If you got poop on any other surface you wouldn't just wipe it off, you'd wash it. Your butt deserves the same dignity'. Dave Praeger makes a similar argument for bidets in *Poop Culture*. Characterizing Americans as 'bathroom Luddites', he notes, 'Given an American obsession with cleanliness that far exceeds most European standards, it's odd that we haven't embraced bidets wholeheartedly. It is inconsistent with general practice: if you got poop on your arm, you'd wash it off, not smear it off. And yet, for the butt, we're content to smear'.***

---

*A good example is the 'Dump on Trump' toilet paper that had a brief spurt of popularity following Trump's inauguration, but mostly ended up gathering dust on bathroom shelves. The symbolism of 'dumping' on Trump is countered by the symbolism of using Trump's face to clean one's arse.

**However, it's worth noting that there are differences in wiping methods between Anglophone countries. Praeger reports that Americans are more likely to be scrunchers and Smyth reports that Brits are more likely to be folders, leading to consumption rates amongst Americans that are double those of their British counterparts. That said, I'm not convinced that folding results in a more economic use of toilet paper. Unlike me, my husband is a folder rather than a scruncher, but because he once saw a programme stating that nine layers are required to ensure that the hand remains free of faecal matter, his toilet paper usage greatly exceeds my own.

***Of course, this is because washing has historically required physical contact between the hand and faecal matter. For wipers, this is a

But these critiques are based on the fallacy that arse-cleaning is a purely instrumental act rather than a simultaneously symbolic one. If we were exclusively concerned with physical hygiene, we'd all be squatting to defecate because this position allows the folds of the rectal cavity to be fully open—sitting dramatically increases the inefficiency of the process (both the evacuating and the wiping). But we sit because we perceive it as more *civilized* than squatting, thus countering the *incivility* of the act of defecation itself. Sitting allows us to maintain the illusion that we might be at a desk reading philosophy rather than ignominiously dumping the contents of our bowels into a porcelain bowl. Squatting, on the other hand, can mean little else (at least to jaundiced Western eyes).

In sum, toilet paper is never *just* toilet paper. It is, as Otsuki observes, the talisman that allows us to cross the treacherous symbolic terrain of defecation—terrain that became particularly (ahem) loaded in Western contexts, where notions of civility were accompanied by a disavowal of our most basic biological attributes. The primary purpose of toilet paper is to mediate between the clean and the dirty; in Otsuki's words, 'We value toilet paper so highly because we sacrifice its cleanliness each day to ensure our own'. This is precisely what Covid revealed: the immense symbolic significance of toilet paper in keeping dirt and disorder at bay. These ideas are so deeply embedded that they resist calls to reduce the business of bum-cleaning to

---

key benefit of toilet paper: the barrier it poses[†] (at least symbolically) between the hand and bodily excreta. Japanese-style toilets with built-in squirters and airers overcome the problem entirely, which probably explains their growing popularity amongst the rich and famous. Indeed, an article in *The Japan Times* reports that the Covid pandemic dramatically bolstered sales of Toto electronic washlet toilets in the USA.

[†]In this respect, it functions much like facial tissues.

its purely instrumental and hygienic dimensions. For most of us, if you want our bog roll, you'll have to pry it from our cold, dead hands.

4

Going to the Dentist Bites

I have always thought I had good, strong teeth. The only braces that have ever come near my mouth were to fix a pronounced cross-bite,* and while my siblings suffered through fillings during their teen years, I remained smugly cavity-free. In fact, one dentist in Australia told me as a teenager that my teeth were so healthy that I didn't need to come back for another ten years—advice I took quite literally. But when I moved to Vancouver in my early thirties, I learned that my 'good' Australian teeth were fundamentally lacking by Canadian standards.** Clearly of the opinion that Australia was some sort of dental backwater,

---

*When I was growing up in regional Australia, braces were an aid to severely crooked teeth. For the dentists who visited schools in mobile dental vans in the 1980s, only the kids who looked like they'd repeatedly been punched in the mouth were considered genuine candidates for braces.

**Still faithfully following the advice of my Australian dentist, I didn't visit a dental clinic when I lived in the USA, but I assume that my experience there would have been like Canada. My first adult trip to the dentist occurred when I was twenty-eight, living in Sydney, and suffering from a toothache, and gave me no reason to believe that my first dentist had been wrong.

my Canadian dentist set about attempting to rectify what she saw as decades of personal and professional neglect.

My wisdom teeth, which had never come through, needed to be pulled; my 'primitive' Australian fillings, which appalled her, had to be replaced; and a pricey mouth guard was prescribed for my nightly grinding. From the first visit, it was also clear that the dentist had an eye toward improving the aesthetic appearance of my teeth. You see, given my steadfast avoidance of whitening products, along with my abiding love of tea, my 'ivories' are actually ivory.* Moreover, they are slightly crooked, and one of my front teeth has a small chip—a defect she immediately noticed on her first examination. 'What are you going to do about your front tooth?', she queried. Slightly nonplussed, I responded defensively, 'I have no problem with it. I quite like it, in fact.' Eye roll. Sigh. She'd clearly seen my type before. 'And anyway,' I added, 'why is it a problem?' 'Well,' she responded, 'It impedes the perfect functioning of your teeth.' I believed I laughed at that point on the premise

---

*The use of 'ivories' as a synonym for teeth speaks to how recent the fixation with whiteness is. I suspect that one of the reasons why the term has fallen out of use is that ivory, with its distinctly yellow undertones, is an increasingly undesirable colour for teeth. For example, the US dental scholar Maura Slack and her colleagues note that while American adults are preoccupied with tooth colour and tooth alignment, children's preferences for white teeth are even stronger—research suggests that most American children think their teeth are too yellow and are more critical of their own tooth colour than their parents and dentists. One just needs to look at the changes in Tom Cruise's teeth over the course of his forty-year filmography to chart the cultural shift towards straight, blindingly white teeth (watch *The Outsiders*, *Top Gun*, and *Mission Impossible: Ghost Protocol* back-to-back for a striking illustration). Interestingly, despite the amount of dental work Cruise has had done, his choppers are still seen to be shy of perfection because of the lack of symmetry of his two front teeth; his so-called 'middle tooth' has been the source of much media discussion.

that she was joking—a fatal error, as it turns out, for I had unwittingly identified myself as an Unrepentant Sinner.

In 1956, the anthropologist Horace Miner observed in a satiric article on the cultural mores of Americans that the 'Nacirema' (American spelt backwards) were obsessed with arresting the natural decay of the body and placed an almost religious faith in 'holy mouth men' to stop the passage of time. To quote Miner:

> The Nacirema have an almost pathological horror of and fascination with the mouth, the condition of which is believed to have a supernatural influence on all social relationships. Were it not for the rituals of the mouth, they believe that their teeth would fall out, their gums bleed, their jaws shrink, their friends desert them, and their lovers reject them. They also believe that a strong relationship exists between oral and moral characteristics.

During my time in Vancouver, I came to appreciate Miner's observation about the ritualistic and moralistic aspects of North American dentistry because my dentist's office had the air of a place of worship. Like any church, pictures of the object of devotion adorned the office walls: the white, straight teeth of salvation and the horribly decayed teeth of the damned—a warning of the dangers of failing to abide by the ritual ablutions (regular brushing, flossing, mouthwash, etc.) prescribed by the dentist.

The tutting would start as soon as I sat in the chair and opened my mouth, first from the patronizingly perky dental hygienist: 'I see that you haven't been flossing regularly.' (What gave it away? Was it the raw gums from two days of intensive flossing in the hopes of making up for six months of laxity?) 'Have you been using that special mouthwash I told you about?' (At twelve dollars a pop, I'd rather spend the money on a bottle of wine, thank you very much.) Then the dentist would arrive, and the chastisement started all over again—this time, the dentist/ high priest would dig around in my mouth and confirm the worst fears of her hygienist/handmaiden. Prodding each tooth, she would call out a series of numbers* to the hygienist: 'Two, three, three, four, five. Oh dear, another five.' I quickly learned the hard way that anything above a four led to a lengthy lecture and appointment slips requesting even more frequent trips to the dentist's office.

I have a theory that North American dentists are almost universally feared not because of the torture they inflict upon our mouths but due to the shame they inflict upon our consciences. This is because good dentists, like priests, trade in guilt. However, there's no quick fix for the sins of poor dentition, no dental equivalent of a Hail Mary that might return one to a state of grace. There's only the long, hard road to salvation: sonic toothbrushes, regular flossing, braces, teeth-whitening treatments, veneers, dental bonding, mouth guards, fluoride treatments, etc. For my dentist and her hygienist, not wanting to have the best teeth you can was akin to not wanting to be a better person. They were, therefore, evangelical in their desire to show me the error of my ways and embrace the dazzling-toothed me I could be.**

This moral dimension of North American dentistry is

*These numbers are gum pocket measurements, which are used to measure periodontal disease. There's no question that large gum pockets hasten tooth loss and decay, but it's also a fact that periodontal pockets naturally increase as we age. Oh, and gum inflammation—of the kind you get from, say, two days of intensive flossing prior to a visit to the dentist—can artificially inflate your measurements, which is why they're only one indicator of gum health.

**They also offered Botox and Restylane injections alongside their regular dental services, in case patients wanted to match their dazzling white teeth with artificially unlined skin.

implicitly highlighted in the work of Penn Handwerker and Stanton Wolfe, a respective anthropologist and dentist who have studied cultural conceptions of 'good' and 'bad' teeth in the USA. Handwerker and Wolfe found that while their interviewees often highlighted the pain, lost time, and financial costs of going to the dentist, a consistent discussion point was their sense of induced embarrassment and defensiveness in response to the criticisms they received regarding their care of their teeth. Indeed, one woman in the study described a recent 'good' dental visit as one in which 'I wasn't yelled at for supposedly not flossing.' (I hear you, sister.) Moreover, they also found that 'good' and 'bad' teeth were defined—by both patients *and* dental professionals—in purely cosmetic terms. This cultural model of bad teeth, Handwerker and Wolfe suggest, is remarkably uniform across gender, social class, and ethnicity, thereby explaining the class divide in oral health. Because bad teeth are viewed as a cosmetic issue, the poorer one is, the less likely they are to prioritize their teeth. Without exception, Handwerker and Wolfe found that people who reported having had bad teeth earlier in life, but good teeth now, explained this by reference to a change in perspective on their future, which they saw as dependent on achieving and maintaining a good appearance.

Observers have commented on the social significance of straight, white teeth for Americans since the early twentieth century. For example, an S.S. White toothpaste advertisement in 1918 (see figure 5) includes a short article from the *Daily Mail* titled 'U.S. Teeth' that begins: 'One thing about the American soldiers and sailors must strike English people when they see these gallant fighters, and that is the soundness and general whiteness of their teeth. It is all the more striking in that it is such a contrast to the teeth of the British people'.

Figure 5. S.S. White toothpaste advertisement, 1918

An illustration of the singular importance Americans attach to straight teeth can be found in a 1950s survey conducted by the sociologist Erwin Linn. Of the 1,862 respondents, the majority rated dental appearance as 'very important' in dating, running for public office, making friends, and getting a job; only 15% or less said that it 'does not matter' or is 'hardly important'. But perhaps most remarkable to cultural outsiders are the answers Linn received when he asked respondents to imagine a hypothetical problem involving 'the Green family'. In the scenario presented, the Green family were saving money to buy a house and had finally found a home they liked in the right price range, but their thirteen-year-old son had become self-conscious about his crooked teeth. A dentist assured the parents that he could fix the son's teeth, but the procedure would use up most of their savings and they would no longer be able to afford the deposit on the house.* Respondents were asked whether the Green family should go ahead and buy the house or have the son's teeth straightened. Eighty per cent (yes, you read that right) said the family should have the son's teeth straightened; notably, the most common reason given was the boy's sensitivity, embarrassment, or self-consciousness. In other words, although the respondents perceived the problem as one of aesthetics rather than oral health, it *still* trumped purchasing a family home.**

The Canadian dental scholars Abeer Khalid and Carlos Quiñonez have highlighted the cultural distinctiveness of the North American model of 'good' teeth—especially the extreme emphasis on white, straight teeth in the USA and Canada. 'The British', they observe, 'view the American smile as unnaturally uniform, artificial, and often vain'. Other countries are far more tolerant of crooked teeth—perhaps most famously Japan, which came to global attention in 2013 due to a new cosmetic dental craze. According to media reports, young women were going to dental clinics to have artificial canines glued to their teeth, giving the appearance of snaggle teeth, or *yaeba*, which are

---

*I'm not sure whether this means that the price of braces was obscenely high, or the cost of housing was ridiculously cheap.

**Given the vague sense of resentment my sister and I felt when we couldn't go to Disneyworld because our eight-year-old brother was hospitalized in the middle of our trip (he had undiagnosed type I diabetes and was extremely sick), I can only speculate on how any hypothetical Green siblings might have felt about their brother's non-medically-related issue being prioritized over a family home.

culturally associated with youthfulness and natural beauty in Japan.

Dentists quickly got in on the act, with one enterprising clinic auditioning girls for a snaggle-tooth girl band, TYB48—a play on AKB48, a highly successful J-pop girl band featuring Tomomi Itano, whose own snaggle tooth was much admired. However, the fake snaggle tooth trend was relatively short-lived, and Japan's love affair with crooked teeth also seems to be waning.* A recent article in *Kyodo News* suggests that 'more and more Japanese are seeking out that winning smile achieved by straightening up', pointing to the significant increase in children's orthodontic clinics in Tokyo. The title of a recent book by Japanese orthodontist Yuki Miyajima suggests the likely roots of this growing preoccupation with straight teeth. Loosely titled in English: *'Polish' Your Teeth Rather Than Your English to Become Cosmopolitan! Dental Care for Being Globally Active*, in an accompanying interview, Miyajima 'vividly remembers the dazzling smiles and pearly whites of the people he would see when he would visit the United States at Saint Louis University, where his father was teaching orthodontics as a visiting professor'.

Despite the evidence of intriguing differences in cultural ideals regarding teeth, Khalid and Quiñonez note that teeth have largely been overlooked by anthropologists and sociologists. This oversight becomes even more remarkable given the widespread symbolic significance of teeth.** Indeed, I can think of few rituals more exotic than

---

*In the event that Tomomi Itano's snaggle tooth can be treated as a proxy for Japanese attitudes towards crooked teeth, it's probably worth noting that it is noticeably less crooked these days.

**In his nineteenth-century opus, *The Golden Bough*, the Scottish anthropologist James Frazer highlighted the ritual meaning frequently attached to teeth. According to his description of sympathetic magic, the practice of encouraging children to place their baby teeth under their pillow or in a glass of water beside their bed so that a supernatural entity can visit when they're sound asleep, taking their teeth for purposes that are entirely unknown, but leaving cold, hard cash in return.* Yet, while 'dental anthropology' constitutes a distinct subfield, it is peopled exclusively by biological anthropologists interested in what teeth can tell us about hominid evolution, physical variation, and the health of past populations.

Clearly, the biological dimensions of teeth are an important part of their significance. As Khalid and Quiñonez suggest, some of the meanings associated with straight, white teeth might relate to the biological messages they convey. Given that various health conditions, along with the ageing process, lead to tooth discolouration and decay, white teeth become a way of faking youth and health, with the social meaning taking its cue from the biological one. As I noted in in 'For the Love of Toilet Paper', white also has broader symbolic associations with cleanliness and purity, especially in Christianity. But it would be a fundamental error to assume that the cultural obsession of North Americans with white, straight teeth is natural (or

---

objects take on magical significance based on either physical resemblance (the Law of Similarity) or prior physical connection (the Law of Contact or Contagion). Teeth and hair fall into the latter category and must often be disposed of carefully, lest they fall into the wrong hands.

*The Tooth Fairy has received little attention from anthropologists; however, folklorists such as Rosemary Wells and Tad Tuleja have shown that the Tooth Fairy is a distinctively American creation, dating to the turn of the twentieth century, but becoming a widespread custom in the post-war period. According to Tuleja, the Tooth Fairy combines British, Irish, and European folk traditions regarding the significance of baby teeth and those highlighting the propensity of fairies and pixies to steal human children and replace them with changelings. This puts a rather more sinister slant on the Tooth Fairy, who is presumably tricked into taking the tooth rather than the child.

healthy*). As Khalid and Quiñonez observe, dental modifications historically abounded in non-Western contexts, including filing, inlays, and teeth-blackening practices—traditionally widespread throughout Southeast Asia and Melanesia.**

According to Thomas Zumbroich, the anthropologist who has most extensively documented teeth-blackening practices, the procedure was performed for various reasons relating to its complex symbolic associations, aesthetic qualities, and perceived health benefits. For example, on Luzon, the largest island in the Philippines, archaeological evidence suggests that tooth-blackening practices date back to at least the fifteenth century. Most of the evidence regarding these practices comes from Spanish missionaries, who were not, to put it mildly, fans of intentionally blackened teeth—or the other forms of dental modification

---

*This speaks to the ways that improving the body's appearance is often conflated with improving health. The great irony, of course, is that the contemporary look of health is often achieved by a cadre of beautification practices that promote the very opposite, such as teeth whitening, tanning, and extreme dieting.

**According to numerous apocryphal accounts, the British nobility had its own brief flirtation with teeth blackening during the reign of Queen Elizabeth I, whose oral health was notoriously bad. The story enters speculative territory with the assertion that the Queen's black and decaying teeth stemmed from her abiding love of sugar and seems to arrive at Evidence-Free Island with the claim that it became fashionable for upper-class women to emulate her blackened teeth as a sign of their social status (sugar being a rare and costly commodity at the time). While of dubious origin, these stories suggest that short-lived cosmetic dental fads are hardly the exclusive province of teenage Japanese girls. It would be a true testament to the power of online influencers such as the Kardashians if one is successfully able to reintroduce tooth-blackening practices. However, based on the ways in which body and beauty norms have shifted radically with the rise of social media (including the rise of 'duck' face, extreme hourglass figures, etc.), I have little doubt that it's possible.

present in the region, such as tooth filing and gold inlays. While locals considered black teeth to be beautiful and healthy, and both men and women engaged in the practice, Spanish colonizers saw these modifications as barbaric, based on the ways they interfered with God-given shape and colour. Locals, in turn, appear to have been equally disgusted by European teeth, with Europeans frequently characterized as 'barbarians' with 'blemished' white teeth.

In various parts of Melanesia, blackened teeth were likewise considered superior to white teeth, although embedded in different ritual beliefs and practices. For example, according to Zumbroich, teeth blackening was performed in the Solomon Islands after puberty on both men and women. The procedure was thought to preserve the teeth and strengthen the gums; however, it was also considered aesthetically pleasing—'teeth like black beetle' was a compliment. For the Rauto of New Britain, an island off the coast of the Papua New Guinean mainland, teeth blackening was an element of male puberty rites and had strong symbolic associations. As white was the colour of sexual aggression and anger, ridding oneself of white teeth demonstrated acceptance of the social norms of Rauto society. For the Rauto, white teeth belonged to the realm of inhuman, uncultured spirits; thus, moral transgressions had the potential to turn teeth white again. Visibly blackened teeth were therefore a physical assertion of an individual's moral development and character. However, these practices had largely died out by the middle of the twentieth century due to missionization. To quote Zumbroich, 'In the eyes of Western missionaries, blackened teeth affirmed every prejudice against Indigenous peoples as dark, dirty and unkempt'.

Yet, while Western missionaries perceived the process of teeth blackening to be ugly and unnatural, the dentist and anthropologist Howard Bailit has suggested that teeth blackening actively protected against periodontal disease. In a 1960s study, he found that dental cavities differed markedly between two neighbouring groups in the Solomon Islands: the Kwaio and the Nasioi. The only difference he could observe was that the Kwaio blackened their teeth and the Nasioi didn't. Zumbroich has likewise compiled extensive evidence suggesting that teeth blackening had a beneficial effect on oral health due to the benefits of covering teeth enamel, and the nature of the substances employed in the process. However, he emphasizes that any medical benefits can't be disentangled from the symbolic and social meanings of the practice. In his words, 'teeth blackening must be recognized as a complex phenomenon, of which the medical aspect is but one significant component inextricably interwoven with other cultural constructs'. The point, of course, holds equally true for North American dental practices, some of which—such as excessive tooth whitening—actively serve to undermine oral health.

As the North American ideal has taken hold globally, and tooth straightening and whitening have become commonplace in other Western countries and beyond, teeth are no longer the marker of national identity that they once were—at least for those under the age of forty. But subtle cultural differences remain, as anyone who has lived inside as well as outside North America will know. For example, in his 'Dentists without Borders' essay, the American humourist David Sedaris provides an entertaining discussion of his experiences with French dentists, who treated his insistence on flossing and request for braces as the personality quirks of a borderline hypochondriac. Although my dentist here in London is not quite so laissez-faire as Sedaris's French dentist, she is worlds away from my dentist in Vancouver. Thus, while my 'good' Australian teeth might have received a failing grade in Canada, it turns out that all I had to do was move to the UK, where I am now the possessor of *amazing* teeth.*

*When I submitted the original essay to the *Globe & Mail*, I included a variation of this sentence, suggesting that my teeth were probably a medical marvel in the UK (the joke that was purely hypothetical at that point, as my move to London didn't occur until years later). The section editor removed the line at the copy-edit stage on the basis that it was offensive to Brits,† and was unmoved by my rejoinder that I was pretty sure the editorial correction said more about Canadian sensibilities than British ones. Thus, the original published essay ends—very lamely in my view—with the line, 'While my teeth might receive a failing grade in Canada, they are healthy by Australian standards'.

†If the section editor was genuinely concerned about the offence the essay might cause, then the group she should have been worried about was dentists, because I received an irate letter from the president of an academy of cosmetic dentistry shortly after the essay was published informing me that I was going to end up with my teeth in a glass on my bedside table unless I started listening to my dentist.

5

Laundry Location, Location, Location

After my husband and I moved to London, there was one question we repeatedly had cause to ask ourselves as we were looking for a place to live: why do Brits insist on putting their washing machines in their kitchens? It didn't seem to matter how old the property was or how large; the washing machine was usually in the kitchen. The complaint is a common one amongst expats living in the UK. As Tanya Vincent, an Australian architect living in London, observed in *The Guardian* more than fifteen years ago: 'The washing machine in the kitchen is a convention so entrenched that it is barely questioned. Granted, British houses don't all have the luxury of a utility room, but what's often required is a more realistic allocation of space. A family house with three bathrooms but no utility room is not balanced: one could easily be converted'. In the end, putting it down to a quirk of British life, we resigned ourselves to the inevitability of purchasing a house with a washing machine in the kitchen, although we quickly moved it to what had been a completely unnecessary downstairs shower room.

Although expats seem to get away with questioning

this practice, similar observations by television personality Kirstie Allsopp of *Location, Location, Location* fame received a very different reception. In 2017, Allsopp inadvertently set off a Twitter storm* in her response to a tweet by the journalist Jim Waterson, who had noted, 'Americans in our office are always confused by the British habit of putting washing machines in kitchens and view this as disgusting'. Allsopp responded, tongue half-in-cheek, 'It is disgusting, my life's work is in part dedicated to getting washing machines out of the kitchen'. The response was immediate and irate, with British tweeters demanding to know where washing machines should be put if a homeowner has no utility room. Allsopp's reaction, 'Bathroom,** hall cupboard, airing cupboard', merely inflamed the Twitter mob and death threats ensued.*** Out of patience, Allsopp noted in her closing salvo, 'Look you bunch of total fuck wits, IF POSSIBLE have a washing machine out of the kitchen frees up space, if not possible no big deal'.

For many Brits, Allsopp's reflections on washing ma-

---

*Although let's face it, it doesn't take much.

**UK building regulations for electrical wiring are sometimes used as an explanation for the ubiquity of washing machines in kitchens and their relative absence in bathrooms. For example, the most popular response to the Reddit thread 'Why do people in the UK typically have their washing machine (for clothes) in the kitchen?', suggests that it's illegal to have electrical outlets in bathroom. It's certainly true that British codes are bewilderingly restrictive on this front in comparison to Australia, which has the same voltage; however, if there is enough distance between the wet zone and the power outlet, you can install a washing machine—a German colleague did this in her bathroom, much to the bemusement of her plumber. Interestingly, the same Reddit thread makes clear the cultural nature of the British preference for washing machines in kitchens when one British respondent notes in passing, 'Washing machines in bathrooms just seems weird'.

***I don't actually know if she got death threats, but we're talking about Twitter, so I can only assume she did.

chines had revealed her to be completely out-of-touch with the lives of regular British people.* 'A posh flat, a holiday cottage, a mansion staffed by six... welcome to the wonky world of Kirstie Allsnob' was the title of a snarky article in the British tabloid *The Sun* by the radio presenter Julia Hartley-Brewer. 'Forget everyone else's dirty laundry, Kirstie, it's time you washed away your own ridiculous privilege', Hartley-Brewer intoned in the piece. Even *Buzz-Feed* had a writeup on the spat, titled 'It's time to accept that British people are right, your washing machine should be in the kitchen'.** YouGov, the influential British survey website, rapidly developed the following poll:

> Location, Location, Location host Kirstie Allsopp has come under fire for agreeing with a view attributed to American workers in London that the British habit of putting washing machines in kitchens is 'disgusting'. Asked to suggest places a washing machine could go in a home without a utility room, Allsopp suggested the bathroom, hall cupboard, airing cupboard or a 'tiny laundry room'. Do you think the kitchen is or is not the right place to have a washing machine?

They surveyed 3,641 adults and 67% of respondents indicated that the kitchen was indeed the right place to have the washing machine. The proportions remained similar regardless of political affiliation and demograph-

---

*Allsopp comes from British nobility and is technically The Honourable Kirstie Allsopp. However, attacks attributing her comments to class privilege seem a little odd, given that her opinion is one shared by tens of thousands of expats living in the UK.

**Given that the publication is read by a primarily American audience, this strikes me as a rather bizarre position to take, but the author's argument seems to be that having a washing machine in one's kitchen is better than not having a washing machine at all, which was never actually in dispute.

ic characteristics, although Liberal Democrats, men, and people over twenty-four were somewhat less likely to agree. British people, it seemed, had definitively spoken: washing machines belong in kitchens.

Brits will generally tell you that washing machines are placed in kitchens purely because of utilitarian considerations relating to the age of most properties: constraints on plumbing and space issues are the usual talking points. For example, in her takedown of Allsopp, Hartley-Brewer states, 'Like pretty much everyone else in Britain I keep my washing machine where God intended—in the kitchen. Why? Because, like pretty much everyone else in Britain, I don't have anywhere else to put it'. However, to most foreigners, this explanation seems inadequate. While it's true that the square footage of the average-size home is markedly larger in North America and Australia than in the UK,* even in cities where space is at a premium, architects still find room for laundry areas, which are often placed in closets near bathrooms—or occasionally in bathrooms themselves. Of course, housing is typically newer in these countries, but washing machines tend to be placed in kitchens in the UK regardless of the property's age. Moreover, even in properties that have been extensively renovated, with loft extensions and extra bathrooms added, washing machines still tend to be placed in kitchens.

This is probably what foreigners find most bewildering

*A 2017 Point2Homes survey found that Australians have the largest homes in terms of square footage, and Americans the second largest; however, Americans enjoy the most living space per person. In other words, their living space is the largest when the number of occupants is considered. According to the survey, UK home sizes are, on average, 20% smaller than those of Americans. In terms of living area per person, the USA and Canada are first and second, respectively, followed by Australia. The UK comes in sixth, after Germany and France.

about British attitudes to washing machines: even when people have the option to place their washing machine elsewhere, they seem to prefer the kitchen; this is effectively what the YouGov survey found. The standard British position on washing machines wouldn't be so odd from the point of view of expats living in the country if it had no knock-on effects; however, placing the washing machine in the kitchen often precludes the possibility of a dryer.* As Corinne Purtill notes of Brits' seeming indifference to installing dryers:

> To an American, this is baffling. Britain is not sunny Italy, where I'm guessing you can simply fling washed clothes onto the *terrazza* in the morning and they're crisp by the end of your post-prandial nap. Britain is damp. It's wet all the time. It rained every single day for a month when I first moved there—and that was in the summer. It is a place crying out for the convenience of warm, dry clothes.

The damp climate means that people are forced to use a drying rack, thus taking up precious real estate in the kitchen or living room while simultaneously requiring that clothes are draped all over the radiators and chairs. Alternatively, you can purchase a combined washer/dryer in place of a washing machine, which is what our house came equipped with. While it *sounds* like a viable solution to the problem, this godawful device takes a tiny volume of clothes, washes them badly, and dries them until they

---

*I'm not suggesting that a dryer is always necessary. They weren't common in Australia when I was growing up either, but it was Australia and I lived in Queensland, a.k.a. the *Sunshine State*. Even self-declared 'dyed-in-the-wool' Europeans who typically shun decadent American appliances like tumble dryers can see their appeal. As Jessica Furseth acknowledges, 'Britain is a very damp island, and air-drying laundry in winter can take days'.

squeak* but are not dry enough to, you know, actually fold up and put away. Oh, and the whole process takes about five hours. As Purtill notes of her experience, 'I was happy living in London, except when I did my laundry, when I would, for an angry moment, will the entire bloody island to sink into the sea'. Faced with the daily frustrations it entails, the British insistence that washing machines belong in kitchens starts to seem like a curious sort of cultural blindness.**

As the anthropologist Irene Cieraad notes: 'The reasons for the characteristics of our domestic surroundings seem self-evident, preventing us from asking such obvious questions as: Why do we cover our interior walls and windows? Why is it that we seldom put a bed in the kitchen? Why store dirty laundry in hidden corners?' According to Cieraad, the answers to these questions are never just about aesthetic or hygienic considerations; rather, home architecture provides a symbolic expression of cultural values. As anthropologists, sociologists, and human geographers have long intuited, how domestic space is arranged provides us with critical insights into local belief systems and values, along with the social and gender hierarchies

---

*It's very difficult to describe the texture of clothes washed in one of these devices. The only analogy I can think of is that sensation of dryness you get in your mouth when intensely nervous. You know there's saliva in there somewhere, but it seems to have been completely sucked out. That is what clothes feel like—they're still damp but simultaneously lacking in moisture.

**Another culprit may be what the anthropologist Kate Fox has described in *Watching the English* as a 'quintessentially English' mindset, which emphasizes moderation ('What do we want? GRADUAL CHANGE! When do we want it? IN DUE COURSE!') and Eeyorishness (named after Eeyore of *Winnie-the-Pooh* fame, Fox uses it to refer to a sort of chronic pessimism that assumes that it's in the nature of things to go wrong, and getting one's hopes up only leads to disappointment).

they entail.

It's undoubtedly true that the age of British housing is part of the story of why washing machines are generally located in kitchens, but less due to the constraints this placed on the appliance's position and more because of how houses were designed to be used. As the British sociologists Martin Hand, Elizabeth Shove, and Dale Southerton note, most people in the UK live in older houses that were 'designed and built around ideals and practices unlike those that dominate today'. British houses built before the postwar period contain clearly demarcated rooms—the typical home featured a front parlour and a back kitchen, which is still the standard configuration of pre-war properties today. The architect Tanya Vincent observes that many British kitchens remain a separate room where the work surfaces all face the wall, suggesting that this relates to the history of kitchens as a service space and 'originates from the days when ingredients were either freshly killed or covered in soil'. In this context, the kitchen was a logical space for washing clothes because of its role as a service room that dealt in dirt as well as food; indeed, large houses frequently had a scullery explicitly for these combined purposes of washing dishes and laundering clothes.

According to the human geographer Louise Johnson, kitchens in most Western countries were typically located at the back of the house before the 1950s, which related to their lower status as 'spaces dealing with food, dirt, women and servants'. But things changed dramatically with the rise of open-plan living. As the design historian Judy Attfield notes, modernist architects saw open plan as a means of embedding modern values in the house's structure itself. Thus, ease of use and maintenance were prioritized, traditional styles and unnecessary ornamentation were rejected in favour of a minimalist aesthetic, and walls were eliminated to create a more 'democratic' multipurpose living space. A core feature of open planning was the relocation of the kitchen, which became the literal and symbolic core of the home, containing visual sight lines to the key living areas.* This amounted to a radical conceptual rehabilitation of the kitchen itself, which was now conceived as part of a larger 'living' space—except, that is, in the UK.

Although open-plan houses became standard across much of the Western world in the post-war period, they weren't embraced in the UK in quite the same way.** Indeed, you only need to look at representations of quintessentially 'British' interiors to see that dark, cosy rooms have traditionally been favoured over bright, open-plan spaces. An illustration of the British ambivalence towards open plan is evident in the history of New Harlow, discussed in detail by Judy Attfield. New Harlow was a planned community*** developed in the 1950s—a key impetus for its establishment was the need to provide for overspill from London following the Second World War.

---

*This was in part so the mother could keep an eye on the children while cooking meals, thus literalizing the idea that a woman's place is in the home (and, more specifically, the kitchen).

**This is reflected in the differences between Anglophone countries in terms of how they label this space. 'Living room' is standard parlance in North America, and widely used in Australia, although 'lounge room' is still common in the latter. However, in the UK, the terminology tends to be more specific. Brits generally prefer terms such as 'lounges', 'parlours', and 'sitting rooms' over 'living rooms'. Indeed, in *Watching the English*, Kate Fox suggests that it's passé for the upper-middle class to use the term 'living room', although they wouldn't be caught dead saying 'lounge' either, which has working class connotations.

***This is always a bad sign, as anyone who's ever been to Canberra can attest. For those who've never visited the city, Bill Bryson's slogans in *In a Sunburned Country* sum it up nicely: 'Canberra—There's Nothing to It!', 'Canberra—Why Wait for Death?', and 'Canberra—Gateway to Everywhere Else!'

The city planners and architects aimed to impose modern 'good design' ideals in the town planning and the layout of the council housing that predominated. Most New Harlow houses contained an open-plan living space instead of the usual two reception rooms—the architects saw this as democratizing the space by dissolving the 'cold formality' of the front room and the 'unquestioned traditional social hierarchy' on which it rested. The tenants, however, hated it. The disappearance of the wall separating the front room from the back meant that there was no longer a physical separation between the 'parlour'—typically kept tidy and the space where guests were received—from the more private, everyday activities in the back of the house.

If, as the anthropologist Kate Fox has suggested, English-ness is characterized by an almost pathological need for privacy, the disappearance of the front room was no minor loss because the 'public' living area at the front of the house had become inseparable from the 'private' living spaces at the back. Tenants reacted to this attempt to kill off the parlour by trying to recreate it. They constructed net curtains to create separate spaces and used furniture to differentiate the front 'room' from the back and the kitchen from the dining area. In some instances, they made illegal modifications, making structural alterations to add and reposition walls. The architects, in their turn, were bitterly resentful that their efforts to create new, more spacious accommodations were unappreciated by tenants. They complained that 'open-plan houses are being closed up again, light rooms are darkened and a feeling of spaciousness is reduced to cosy clutter'. In New Harlow's tower blocks, the problems in flats were even more acute because of their smaller size. Tenants' primary objection was the lack of space to accommodate kitchen appliances, including refrigerators and washing machines. Prospective

Figure 6. Sofa/buggy symbol on real estate listings

tenants were told to keep their fridges in the hall and their washing machines on the balcony. According to Attfield, this caused considerable indignation because residents were being asked to place their appliances in 'inappropriate' living spaces.

Although attitudes towards open-plan living have unquestionably changed over the past fifty years, the imprint of these earlier cultural preferences is evident in the way properties are currently marketed in the UK. My husband and I discovered this the hard way when we moved to London. We noticed that property listings were accompanied by an odd-looking symbol (see figure 6) that clearly meant something significant, although we weren't sure what.* My husband thought the symbol looked like a sofa, but I figured it must be an old-fashioned buggy that designated the property's number of parking spots.** However, I quickly became annoyed during viewings because few of the houses had designated parking. 'This is false

---

*Today, this symbol is clearly identified as a reception room on most real estate websites, perhaps because of all the confused foreigners looking to purchase housing in London, but this wasn't the case when we moved to the UK.

**Sometimes there was one buggy symbol, but often two, and sometimes three, although that seemed an excessive number of car spots to me.

advertising,' I ranted to my husband after our fifth viewing in which the property had no parking spot, despite the two buggy symbols prominently featured on the listing. Finally, we thought to ask an estate agent what the symbol meant. It was, he affirmed, a sofa and indicated how many reception rooms the property had. As Australians who had lived in Canada for over a decade, and with open-plan layouts standard in both countries, this emphasis on reception rooms was utterly meaningless to us. 'Why on earth would anyone care how many reception rooms they had?', we wondered.* This was our first indication that the features valued in London properties differed from our prior experiences in Canada, where reception rooms were non-existent and parking spots standard.

Over time, open-plan living has become more normalized in the UK. For instance, it's common for the wall between the two reception rooms to be removed—at least partially—although they are still generally treated as separate rooms in real estate listings. However, the view of kitchens as exclusively service spaces has arguably lingered until relatively recently. In their 2007 study of UK home extensions, Hand and colleagues highlighted various renovation trends in the UK, including the rise in the number of bathrooms, the decline of the separate dining room, and the growing use of kitchens as living spaces. In their words: 'The kitchen has rid itself of certain functions and appliances (such as those associated with the laundry) and acquired others (specifically the dishwasher and the fridge freezer, along with a host of smaller gadgets), and the more important development is the idea that

---

*Although I certainly appreciate the distinction now. Covid lockdowns quickly made us all realize that open-plan living isn't all it is cracked up to be. Interestingly, one of the main post-Covid home renovation trends has been a move away from open-plan layouts.

the kitchen constitutes the symbolic heart of the home'. While Hand and colleagues suggest that these shifts were partially necessitated by the need for washing machines to make way for other appliances such as the dishwasher, the reconceptualization of the kitchen as a *living* space was also critical.

Once the kitchen is no longer merely a service room, this changes how it is conceived and used, including what activities are and aren't considered appropriate. This is why washing machines in kitchens seem odd to most foreigners—living spaces are areas where we relax, socialize, cook, and eat (ideally with the cook able to socialize while preparing food*). They are not the appropriate location to perform ablutions on our bodies or clothes. It's also why this location occasionally attracts disgust amongst those unfamiliar with British norms. When a kitchen is a living space, activities dealing with the body's effluvia suddenly become matter out of place—or, to use Mary Douglas's terminology, 'dirt'. As Douglas notes in *Purity and Danger*: 'Shoes are not dirty in themselves, but it is dirty to place them on the dining-table; food is not dirty in itself, but it is dirty to leave cooking utensils in the bedroom, or food bespattered on clothing... and so on'. Because conceptions of 'dirt' rely on how spaces are classified, reclassifying the space inevitably leads to a reclassification of what is dirty. This comes across strongly in a response Allsopp made to a tweeter demanding to know why washing machines in the kitchen were 'disgusting'. In her words, 'Why does anyone want to mix poo, pee & period with food unless they have to?'

In sum, although British people will repeatedly tell

---

*The conceptual transformation of cooking into a hobby more than a necessity is also part of the shift in the meaning of the kitchen.

you that washing machines, of necessity, are located in kitchens, they are lying—albeit mostly to themselves. The fact is that anyone with the means to renovate a property large enough to contain a washing machine can often put that washing machine somewhere else—and maybe install a dryer to boot! This doesn't mean that washing machines in kitchens are 'disgusting' or 'unhygienic'. Instead, the unquestioned practice of placing them in kitchens is the product of the cultural ideals that British houses embedded, which related to notions of public and private space that have only recently shifted—especially in the context of the meaning and purpose of kitchens. So the next time you hear a British person moaning about their washing, let them know that a brighter (and drier) world is possible. To quote Purtill, 'Some things cannot be fixed. But some things absolutely can. There are so many intractable problems humanity has yet to solve... Drying clothes is not one of them. We've got this one, people!... You have nothing to lose but your damp'.

6

A Slug is a Snail Without a House

Since moving to the UK, I have finally acquired a small garden—something I have lived without for most of my adult life. Having grown up in the Australian tropics, I was more familiar with snakes and cane toads than the scourge of gardeners everywhere: slugs and snails.* However, this lack of exposure has been speedily rectified because it soon became apparent that our tiny backyard was subject to a snail and slug plague of biblical proportions. Each day we were greeted by the sight of glistening trails of crisscrossing slime and the carcasses of overpriced plants from the local nursery.

One weekend, deciding enough was enough, my husband and I committed what I'm pretty sure can be characterized as a wanton act of snail slaughter. After reading up on how to get rid of slugs and snails, armed with a spray bottle of vinegar and a bucket of heavily salted water, we went to the garden to finish them off. More than seventy

---

*There are plenty of snails and slugs in the Australian tropics, but they are mostly confined to the rainforest, and aren't generally considered to be garden pests.

slug and snail deaths later, and having witnessed the death throes of dozens, I was convinced, like many of my internet brethren, that they are basically the same creature. As far as I could see, the only difference was the shell, which, in any case, the snails seemed to divest themselves of in their final moments.*

I somewhat unwisely made this observation over lunch the following week to a table full of biological anthropologists and zoologists, who proceeded to treat it with all the respect they felt such a statement was due: namely, wholesale derision.** Not one to concede defeat lightly (or at all), I questioned why the snail's 'house' should be the difference that makes a difference, especially when they are otherwise basically identical—from their general shape and size to their eating habits and sexual attributes (both are hermaphrodites). Thus began a protracted debate that ultimately hinged on the relationship between scientific taxonomies and what are generally called folk taxonomies and ethnotaxonomies—those used by ordinary people and those used in other cultures, respectively, to describe their natural surroundings.

---

*I will admit to being somewhat confused on this front as online experts like the Snail Wrangler insist that snails can't divest themselves of their shells—although I think we can safely assume that a woman who regularly gives talks on 'marvellous mucus' has never sprayed them with acid and rubbed salt in their wounds (as a colleague described our actions). Thus, while a snail might not be able to *live* without its shell, it follows that it can certainly *die* without it.

**Although the entomologist wasn't surprised. He'd written me off as a hopeless case after I assumed that the springtail† was a bird.

†Springtails are a type of small, insect-like creature, that, rather confusingly, are no longer classified as insects because they have internal rather than external mouthparts. The roving taxonomic status of the springtail is a perfect illustration of the unstable nature of scientific classifications, which I will have more to say on shortly.

In his book *The Order of Things*, the French philosopher Michel Foucault provided what is perhaps the most fantastical and famous example of an ethnotaxonomy. Citing the Argentinian writer Jorge Luis Borges, he quotes 'a certain Chinese encyclopaedia', in which it is written that: 'Animals are divided into: (a) belonging to the Emperor, (b) embalmed, (c) tame, (d) suckling pigs, (e) sirens, (f) fabulous, (g) stray dogs, (h) included in the present classification, (i) frenzied, (j) innumerable, (k) drawn with a very fine camelhair brush, (l) *et cetera*, (m) having just broken the water pitcher, (n) that from a long way off look like flies'. Foucault suggests that in the 'wonderment of this taxonomy', we are confronted with the stark impossibility of reconciling our own system of thought with one that differs radically from it, thereby eluding the possibility of mutual comprehension. However, it's worth noting that many of Borges' works featured pseudo-references that mixed fact and fiction,* so it's not clear that the taxonomy is the product of anything more than the mind of a writer known for his preoccupation with magical realism. Indeed, anthropological work on ethnotaxonomies gives us reason to doubt the veracity of Borges' list because this research suggests that such taxonomies typically entail some engagement with nature on its own terms—at least, for any society wishing to survive long-term.

As the biological anthropologist Kieran McNulty notes, the drive to classify seems to be core to human evolution: it is in our nature to categorize our surroundings. After all, questions like 'Is this safe or not safe to eat?', 'Is that a predator or prey?', and 'Are these kin or potential mates?' entail processes of categorization and classification.

---

*Given that I got this information from Wikipedia, this seems like a pot-meet-kettle situation.

Amongst anthropologists and evolutionary psychologists, there has been considerable interest in cross-cultural universals in ethnotaxonomies and how these speak to the evolution of human cognition. According to the anthropologist Peter Dwyer, this was a major feature of anthropological research on classification as it developed in the 1960s and 70s. The problem is that while naming and classification systems are part of environmentally specific survival strategies, they also serve intellectual ends. As Dwyer observes, classifications speak to our imaginations as well as our observations about the world.

An early attempt to theorize the observational and imaginative aspects of ethnotaxonomies can be found in the 1903 book *Primitive Classification* by the French sociologists Émile Durkheim and Marcel Mauss. They made a distinction between 'technological' classifications, which aim to classify things according to their use, and classifications that have a more speculative purpose, with the object not of facilitating action but advancing understanding. The latter kinds of symbolic classifications, Durkheim and Mauss suggested, effectively constitute a philosophy of nature that aims 'to make intelligible the relations which exist between things'—especially 'totemic' classification systems in which the human and non-human world are conceptualized in relation to each other.* Therefore, things don't present themselves to us arranged in any particular way. According to Durkheim and Mauss, although we may vaguely perceive the resemblances between things, the simple fact of these resemblances isn't enough to explain why we are led to group things, bringing them together in

*Like film critic Roger Ebert's Law of Economy of Characters, this seemingly passing reference to totemic classification will become a whole lot more significant in 'Menageries and Stock Markets'.

an ideal, imagined sphere as a 'class', 'species', etc.

Although Durkheim and Mauss's distinction between technological and symbolic classifications was integral to early anthropological studies of ethnoclassification, the challenge of maintaining clear lines of distinction between these two types are apparent in the anthropologist Ralph Bulmer's influential study of zoological taxonomy amongst the Karam of the Papua New Guinean Highlands. Readers familiar with Jared Diamond may recall Papua New Guinea as the inspiration for *Guns, Germs and Steel*. As Diamond notes, Papua New Guineans have extraordinarily well-honed observation skills about their natural environment. Bulmer found this in his work with the Karam in the 1960s—their 'enormous, detailed and on the whole highly accurate knowledge of natural history'. Such knowledge was reflected in their taxonomy, which focused on physical differences between animals (e.g., bony vs boneless, winged vs wingless, quadrupedal vs bipedal vs limbless), differences in habitat (e.g., forest vs homestead vs gardens), feeding habits, and so on, that broadly corresponded to scientific taxonomies. However, Bulmer observed that at the upper level of the Karam taxonomy, objective biological facts no longer dominated, and cultural beliefs became more significant, allowing 'a far greater, almost infinitely varied set of possibilities'.

The cultural dimension of the Karam's zoological taxonomy was most evident in the taxonomic status of the cassowary—a large flightless bird native to Indonesia, Papua New Guinea, and north-eastern Australia. Picture an ostrich crossed with a hornbill crossed with a parrot, with a tingle of velociraptor thrown in for good measure* (see figure 7). Cassowaries have many qualities that distinguish

---

*The cassowary has the distinction of being the most lethal of all birds.

Figure 7. illustration of a cassowary by Eugene Fornier, 1869

them from other birds: they can't fly, they are virtually wingless, and they are anomalously large—in fact, the largest creature in the Papua New Guinean Highlands aside from humans and pigs. Moreover, although shy and retiring, they can inflict serious wounds if cornered.

In some parts of the Highlands they are recognized as birds, but the Karam place the cassowary in its own taxonomic category. According to Bulmer, if you ask the Karam, they will tell you this is because of the cassowary's distinctiveness. For example, some of his informants told him, 'The cassowary's head is all bone: it has no brain, not like a bird'. However, Bulmer argues that its unique status is explained not just by the cassowary's anomalous features but by its unique relationship with humans. This becomes clear in the elaborate ritual prescriptions regarding how cassowaries should be hunted and killed, and mythologies that endow them with quasi-human status.* Bulmer there-

---

*Picture Big Bird and you start to get the idea. Equally brainless, Big Bird is also endowed with semi-human status. Sadly, he has not yet

fore highlighted the importance of understanding Karam cultural beliefs to make sense of their taxonomic classification system at its higher levels.

The significance of culture to Karam taxonomic classifications and other ethnotaxonomies raises the question of what role, if any, culture plays in scientific taxonomies. Contemporary zoological taxonomy has its roots in the framework developed by the eighteenth-century Swedish naturalist Carl Linnaeus (a.k.a. Carl von Linné*), whose *Systema Naturæ* introduced the world to his system of binominal nomenclature—a fancy way of saying 'a two-part system for devising how things are named'. In this system, each organism is ordered hierarchically into a genus and species based on resemblance—it was Linnaeus who gave humans our name (*Homo sapiens*). Linnaean taxonomy aimed to reveal God's Plan in Nature's System: Linnaeus saw himself as uncovering the intelligible order within nature as the work of a divine creator. As the historian Peter Harrison notes of Linnaeus, 'there is every indication in his writings that he imagined himself to be uniquely, indeed divinely, inspired with taxonomic gifts'.**

Such hubris was not lost on his contemporaries; ac-

---

been killed off,† ritually or otherwise.

†I bet Oscar the Grouch has considered it, though. Has there even been a more annoying *Sesame St* character than Big Bird?

* Much like the Australian actor Simon Baker (a.k.a. Simon Denny, a.k.a. Simon Denny Baker) of *The Mentalist fame*, Carl Linnaeus went by several names. He was born Carl Linné, used Carolus Linnaeus in his professional writings (Carolus was the Latinized version of his name), and received the appellation Carl von Linné when he received a title from King Adolf Frederik—the 'von' was borrowed from German to designate Linnaeus's newly ennobled status.

**In other words, Linnaeus was a Type A personality with a God complex—Linnaeus was apparently fond of saying that 'God created, Linnaeus organized'.

cording to Harrison, Linnaeus was frequently accused of imagining himself to be a 'second Adam'—an appellation coined by one of Linnaeus's contemporaries, the Swiss scholar Abrecht von Haller. Irate that Linnaeus had demoted some of von Haller's species to mere varieties, Von Haller wrote snippily: 'the unbounded dominion which Linnaeus has assumed in the animal reign, must upon the whole appear disgusting to many persons. He considered himself as a second Adam, and gave names to all the animals after their distinctive marks, without ever caring for his predecessors'.

Linnaeus's choices for determining plant taxonomy came under heavy fire from fellow botanists. According to Patricia Fara in *Sex, Botany and Empire*, Linnaeus was accused of building an elaborate structure based on relatively unimportant features. While earlier botanists had grouped plants by characteristics like the shape of their leaves or the colour of their flowers, Linnaeus controversially chose to order plants based on their sexual characteristics instead. In this system, classes were distinguished by the number of 'male' parts (stamens) in each flower, whereas orders in these classes were distinguished by their number of 'female' parts (pistils).

The literary scholar Sam George observes that Linnaeus's terminology was inspired by traditional wedding imagery and marital metaphors permeated his taxonomy. Indeed, some of Linnaeus's descriptions read like scenes from a romance novel (a bad one). One particularly florid example contains a description of flower petals suggesting that they serve as 'bridal beds which the Creator has so gloriously arranged, adorned with such noble bed curtains, and perfumed with so many soft scents that the bridegroom with his bride might their celebrate their nuptials with so much the greater solemnity'. Some of his contemporaries were appalled by the licentiousness of Linnaeus's method, along with the apparent lack of monogamous relationships in the botanical world.*

Linnaeus's introduction of the term 'Mammalia', literally meaning 'of the breast', also raised more than a few eyebrows, given its abrupt departure from the prevailing terminology of the period ('Quadrupedia'). As the historian Lorna Schiebinger notes, although the term Quadrupedia had various problems, the presence of milk-producing mammary glands is one of a variety of characteristics shared by the animals Linnaeus placed in this category. Indeed, others are arguably superior for the purposes of classification, being shared by both sexes and better accounting for egg-laying mammals (e.g., hair). The point is that Linnaeus's taxonomic system involved choices about which features were significant enough to be counted and which weren't important enough to matter—choices that Fara and Schiebinger suggest were embedded in the gender politics of the period. As the sociologists Geoffrey Bowker and Susan Leigh Star observe in *Sorting Things Out: Classification and Its Consequences*, 'each standard and each category valorizes some point of view and silences another'.

Although the framework Linnaeus developed for naming species is still in place, and many of the species Linnaeus named have the same designations today,** contem-

---

*According to George, the outraged German botanist Johann Siegsebeck insisted that God would never have permitted such 'loathsome harlotry' as several males fertilizing one female. Clearly not one to take the moral high ground, Linnaeus responded by naming a genus of weedy, tiny-flowered plants *Siegesbeckia* in honour of his critic. Likewise, the British botanist Charles Alston declared Linnaeus's description of a pansy, with its female parts gaping wantonly below the stamens, 'too smutty for British ears'.

**Hubris aside, this is a remarkable achievement. A study by Young-Ho Eom and his colleagues employing computational and data-mining

porary scientific taxonomies were modified by the work of Charles Darwin. Writing a century later, Darwin saw within Linnaeus's system the underlying bond between organisms that was otherwise hidden by various degrees of physical modification. The subsequent rise of evolutionary theory led to the development of phylogenetic classification, where organisms are arranged based on common ancestry rather than similarity alone, which was Linnaeus's method. This has meant that biological taxonomies constantly change as our understanding of evolutionary history improves.

As Kieran McNulty observes, one only needs to look at the constant reshuffling of the species grouped as part of the family Hominidae to see the ways in which zoological taxonomy is constantly being revised. For example, as genetic evidence showed that humans, chimpanzees, and gorillas were much more closely related than previously assumed, it no longer seemed justifiable to separate them into distinct families. Thus, the family Pongidae, which contained orangutans, gorillas, and chimpanzees, has been abandoned and all great apes (including humans) are now included in the Hominidae. Arguably, this reshuffle isn't merely technical but has affected how we relate to other great apes. As the biological anthropologist Colin Groves noted: 'As knowledge and understanding about the taxonomy of great apes grows, it becomes obvious that great apes—better, "non-human great apes"—are very like humans, not only genetically and anatomically but also cognitively'. This, he suggested, makes it harder to justify their captivity in zoos for the entertainment of humans, except

---

techniques has shown that Linnaeus is the top-ranked historical figure on Wikipedia, rating above Jesus, Aristotle, Napoleon, and Hitler, which I assume would have pleased Linnaeus no end.

under very specific conditions.

Clearly, scientific taxonomies, like symbolic taxonomies, are not merely descriptive but aim to make the relationship between things intelligible; they provide 'a philosophy of nature', to use Durkheim and Mauss's expression. Indeed, Durkheim and Mauss saw symbolic and scientific classification as directly analogous.* However, scientific taxonomies prioritize one kind of classificatory relationship at the expense of all others: ancestry. While that makes sense for understanding the questions scientists are interested in answering about the evolution of life, such taxonomies are less useful in understanding other kinds of relationships we have with the natural world. Here, we turn to folk taxonomies to classify and sort the world around us.

Generally, we pay little attention to folk taxonomies because they are buried in the very language we use to describe the natural world. As the anthropologist Edmund Leach observed, we are taught that the world consists of 'things' distinguished by names. However, the naming process itself is critical to the act of classification because it carves up an otherwise continuous environment into discrete objects. To name something is to classify it: language, in Leach's view, does more than provide us with a classification of things; it actually moulds our environment.

Consider the English word 'snail'.** Etymologically speaking, its roots are in the Proto-Germanic *snagila*, from

---

*These points were later elaborated by the French anthropologist Claude Lévi-Strauss in *The Savage Mind*, where he described mythological thought as a 'science of the concrete' directly analogous to scientific thought. I will have much more to say about Lévi-Strauss in the next two chapters.

**You didn't think I'd forgotten what this chapter is supposed to be about, did you?

snog-, which is a variant of *sneg-*, meaning 'to crawl, creep; creeping thing'. Interestingly, a distinction between 'snails' and 'slugs' wasn't made in English until the 1700s—the former term covered both creatures, which makes sense given the root of 'snail' itself as describing a crawling, creeping thing. However, in the 1700s, 'slug' started to be used as a distinct term for the shell-less land snail—it was borrowed from the term used to describe a lazy person ('slug' is etymologically related to 'sluggard'). Linguistically, then, English tends to emphasize the similarities between snails and slugs over their differences: they are both creeping, crawling creatures, bar the latter's lack of a shell. This linguistic connection is reinforced culturally; for example, according to the kids' version of the online *Encyclopaedia Britannica*, 'Snails and slugs are similar animals. The main difference between them is that a snail has a shell and a slug does not'.* This, I would suggest, is why gardeners so frequently submit Google queries around whether snails and slugs are *actually* different.

If we turn to French, however, a different set of linguistic associations emerge that suggest a rather different cultural relationship with snails and slugs. In French, snails are, of course, *escargot*, which comes from the Latin *conchylium*, meaning 'edible shellfish'. I can personally attest that snails cooked the French way are delicious,** although it is far from the only cuisine to employ gastropods—accord-

---

*The primary distinction is that we use the terms slightly differently when applying them to people—we say that someone is 'sluggish' but not 'snailish', and we talk about people moving at 'snail's pace' rather than 'slug's pace', suggesting that we see snails as slow and slugs as lazy—probably because the latter move slowly, but aren't carrying a house on their back.

**Although I suspect this is primarily to do with the lavish amounts of butter in which they are cooked.

ing to the historian Felipe Fernandez-Armesto, archaeological evidence from Mesopotamian sites suggests that snails were eaten in abundance in ancient Sumer. Regardless, in light of the different linguistic associations of the two terms, it's not much of a surprise that the French were keener to eat snails than the English, given that one language places them in the same category with lobsters and the other with snakes.*

The French term for slugs, on the other hand, is *limace*, which comes from the Latin root *limus*, a figurative term for faeces within the bowels used to describe filth, pollution, mud, slime, and muck. In effect, the linguistic connection between slugs and snails in English is entirely lacking in French. It's therefore not surprising that while the French eat snails, they avoid slugs**—my suspicion is that not even Julia Childs' dictum that 'With enough butter, anything is good' was enough to overcome the linguis-

---

*This immediately begs the chicken and egg question: did the term lead the French to eat snails, or were snails named this *because* they were eaten? Although this is the sort of question philosophers can easily spend hours debating, I suspect it probably misses the point. Bulmer helpfully frames it as the 'chicken vs egg-head' question. In his words, 'It seems probable that the egg-head, a category of domesticated or semi-domesticated human being defined by, among other things, a propensity for theorising about nature and society, arrived first'.

**Based on the number of articles with variants of the title 'How to eat slugs and not die' that show up when you do a search on the edibility of slugs, they are widely believed to be inedible. However, slugs are no more prone to the rat lungworm† parasite than snails. While there are some suggestions that they have a more bitter flavour, I suspect that the presumed inedibility of slugs is primarily a result of their linguistic associations in English and French—although I don't plan to test this theory myself.

†When ingested via the organisms that carry this parasite (including raw slugs and snails), it seems to function much like the Ceti eel in *Star Trek II: The Wrath of Khan*, except it burrows into the cerebral cortex and slowly kills you without making you susceptible to suggestion first.

tic associations between slugs and filth. As Leach observed: 'The physical environment of any human society contains a vast range of materials which are both edible and nourishing, but, in most cases, only a small part of this edible environment will actually be classified as potential food. Such classification is a matter of language and culture, not of nature'.

In sum, whether slugs and snails are basically the same creature depends on what kind of taxonomy you prioritize and what version of 'natural' you employ. According to Ralph Bulmer, a taxonomic group can be natural in a biological or a logical sense insofar as it contains members that possess numerous common attributes. Most taxonomies include various elements that are natural in both senses (bar Borges' dubious 'Chinese encyclopaedia'), but arguably there is no taxonomy where this is uniformly true for all elements—the fact that scientific taxonomies are constantly being revised illustrates the point as much as the anomalous ethnotaxonomic status of the cassowary amongst the Karam. Indeed, while a taxonomy based on ancestry might be helpful for biologists, it's not a particularly useful system outside the rarefied circles of science because it can't tell us the things we actually want to know in everyday life, such as which creatures are edible and which aren't, and which ones are garden pests. Thus, in light of the ways English speakers interact with slugs and snails, the shell itself, well, that's not much of a difference at all—beyond the satisfying sound it makes as you crunch one underfoot in the garden.

7

Must Love Dogs

Some years ago, not long after I moved to Vancouver, I read an issue of the local newspaper devoted, in large part, to dogs. There were articles on dog-naming trends in the province (Fido was out and Max was in!), the best designer crossbreeds (labradoodles rock!) and images of adorable dogs frolicking in a dog park. As someone reasonably new to the city at the time (and, quite frankly, a cat person), it seemed a little odd that a newspaper would chronicle so extensively the lives of the local canine population. But I quickly realized that Vancouverites loved—I mean, *really* loved—their dogs.

Today, doggie spas, accessory shops, and day care services in Vancouver are as ubiquitous as Starbucks coffee shops. Dogs have also encroached on those spaces that used to be exclusively human domains—such as supermarkets, restaurants, pubs, and public transit. There seem to be few places they can't enter.* Banks, clothing shops, offices,

---

*I recall sitting in the waiting area at a medical clinic when a woman entered with a Chihuahua. When her name was called, I expected the receptionist to tell her that she couldn't take the dog into the consultation room, but she carried her dog into the appointment without a

and medical clinics welcome them with open arms. Those commercial establishments that adhere to provincial hygiene regulations do so sheepishly, with cutesy, apologetic signs posted outside. To make up for this egregious act, they invariably have a water bowl placed out the front (and sometimes dog treats), so pet pooches don't feel slighted.

When I moved to London, I looked forward to finally living in a city where I no longer had to share café tables and public transit with pampered pooches. I knew Brits loved their dogs (and the Queen her corgis), but I assumed this was in the absent-mindedly affectionate fashion I had witnessed growing up in regional Australia, where dogs knew their place—and it wasn't at the pub or in a pram.* However, while the UK hasn't quite attained the levels of dog love I witnessed in Vancouver, based on the number of dog-friendly pubs, cafes, and hotels in the country, the canine-ification of public space is clearly a pan-cultural phenomenon.

Countries like the USA and Australia seem to have fallen prey to the same trend, with dog-friendly workplaces on the rise and employers increasingly touting the psychological benefits of dogs in offices. Leading the way is Amazon, which boasts that 'employees share workspace with as many as 7,000 dogs' at its Seattle headquarters. It even employs a 'Woof Pack' manager to ensure that canines are happy.** Moreover, 'support' dogs have become a com-

---

single murmur of disapproval (well, apart from my own).

*Interestingly, there is a growing market for dog strollers and carriers, which manages to take the notion of a 'fur baby' to newly literal levels, while simultaneously defeating the purpose of walking the dog.

**As we know from the exposés on the working conditions in Amazon warehouses, humans don't merit quite the same consideration. Indeed, those employees for whom sharing their office space with 7,000 dogs sounds like the Ninth Circle of Hell have little choice but to comply.

mon sight on planes in the USA, although Australian and British travellers have been spared this dubious pleasure due to stricter flight regulations.* Indeed, it increasingly appears that the rights of dog owners supersede those of mere canineless mortals. For example, many feel entitled to take up the entire footpath when walking their dog—expecting the madding crowds to part like the Red Sea so that their majestic beast may stride, like Moses, through our midst. Like most doting parents, they remain oblivious that others may not share their sentiments. I don't know exactly many Vancouverites have been cornered in lifts by growling, leg-humping Pomeranians** or how many Londoners are now expected to relinquish precious space on public transit for someone's pampered pair of Irish wolfhounds,*** but I suspect they number in the thousands.

To make matters worse, you should never, under any circumstances, openly complain about someone's dog. A politely worded 'Can you please move your dog?' will provoke wholesale condemnation from all those within hearing distance.**** This is because you have just publicly

---

*For many years, passengers on American airlines had to suffer not just emotional support dogs, but a veritable menagerie of animals, including emotional support peacocks, pigs, turkeys, and, in one memorable instance, a miniature horse named 'Flirty'. In 2020, finally deciding enough was enough, the US Department of Transportation narrowed their definition of a support animal and only service dogs 'individually trained to do work or perform tasks for the benefit of a person with a disability' currently qualify for the role.

**I'm talking to you, owners of Peaches. Peaches is a sex-fiend and a sociopath.

***I'm talking to you, posh woman on the tube. Your dogs are entitled arseholes—but I'm guessing that they learned that trait from you.

****Conversely, commenting positively on someone's dog is an instant icebreaker. Vancouverites' and Londoners' reputed coolness towards strangers all but melts in the face of a cute canine.

identified yourself as a member of that contemptible human subspecies: Dog Haters. As a former Amazon employee observes, 'We live in such a dog-adoring culture that it's hard to admit when you aren't totally enamored of them. What you are supposed to feel—what you must always feel—is love'. Thus, to openly confess that you dislike 'man's best friend' is to invite speculation that you are a cold, unfeeling brute. If dogs, as is frequently posited, love us unconditionally, the only morally acceptable response is apparently to love them right back.

Much has been made of this canine capacity for pure love—especially in comparison to cats. To quote Sigmund Freud, 'Dogs love their friends and bite their enemies, quite unlike people, who are incapable of pure love and always have to mix love and hate in their object relations'.* Indeed, for some people, dogs are like humans but *better*: more loyal, dependable, and altogether more lovable. 'The more people I meet, the more I like my dog', t-shirts and bumper stickers proclaim.

Even billionaire hotelier Leona Helmsley, widely known as the 'Queen of Mean', wasn't immune to their charms, cutting two grandchildren out of her will and leaving $12 million to Trouble, her beloved Maltese terrier.** Cats, on the other hand, are perceived, at best, as

---

*The value of Freud's observations on the canine temperament are somewhat diminished by the fact that he exclusively owned chow chows—a dog breed that the psychologist Stanley Coren in *The Intelligence of Dogs* has identified as one of the dumbest† in the world.

†The dumbness of chow chows may be directly related to their deliciousness, given that they were initially bred as a food source in China. As Coren observes, 'who wants smart food?'

**Although the will was contested and Trouble ended up with only $2 million, a significant portion of which went to paying for round-the-clock security, given that Helmsley's bequest made Trouble the most kidnap-prone dog in history.

capricious and mercurial and, at worst, as self-absorbed and aloof. For cat lovers, this is part of their attraction: while dogs are prized for the ways they are like us, cats are adored for the ways they are different.* However, those who dislike cats receive no social censure for their views. Nor do cat lovers expect everyone to share our affection— unlike dog owners, we don't generally rub our pets in everyone's faces.** Indeed, to love cats is to place oneself in the company of crazy old spinsters and Bond-style supervillains.

In *Affect, Imagery, Consciousness*, the psychologist Silvan Tomkins suggested that these different responses of dogs and cats to humans are due primarily to the graded fear and aggression response of the former, in tandem with their enhanced ability to sustain positive affect (i.e., amiability). Cats, according to Tomkins, lack this same gradated emotional range. When provoked, their fear and aggression response remains unmodulated, and their threshold for human companionship and tolerance for physical affection tends to be correspondingly lower than dogs.***

---

*Mark Twain, whose chosen monikers for his many cats included Beelzebub, Blatherskite, Satan, Sin, Sour Mash, and Pestilence, captured this quality nicely in his observation that, 'If man could be crossed with the cat, it would improve man, but it would deteriorate the cat'.

**While cat lovers often choose to display their affections online, the crucial difference is that no one is forced to engage.†

†Saying you 'accidentally' watched cat videos on YouTube is like saying you accidentally watched porn on the internet. Sure, there's millions of clips out there, but doing a Google search on 'Albert Camus' isn't going to bring up that adorable 'Surprised Kitty' video (now with more than 79 million hits on YouTube) or scenes from *Sex Trek: The Next Penetration*, no matter what you tell your partner/mother/roommate.

***As PawTracks puts it, 'They are like little adorable divas that don't seem to know exactly what they want. They purr and rub against you until you pet them, but they'll scratch you out of nowhere when they've had enough'.

These attributes, Tomkins argued, accounted for 'the greater readiness of the dog for domestication' than other animals. Indeed, dogs were the first animal to be domesticated—around 15,000 years ago. But unlike other domestic animals, our relationship with dogs was unique. In *Dogs: Domestication and the Development of a Social Bond*, the archaeologist Darcy Morey notes that it was first and foremost a *social* relationship rather than a *utilitarian* one. While dogs were workers and protectors (and, on occasion, food), they appear to have been valued primarily for their companionship. Evidence of ritualistic burials of dogs abounds, and they were frequently interred on death in a manner similar to family members.

In numerous cultures, dogs hold a unique status in the animal kingdom—deemed to be halfway between animal and human. Consider the Native American Trickster figure, who, while taking various forms, is most frequently represented in the guise of a coyote. In the Winnebago myths detailed by the anthropologist Paul Radin, he is a simultaneously superhuman and subhuman figure of uncontrolled appetites and excesses. Whether it be throwing his detachable penis at a princess he fancies, or eating a laxative bulb that makes him fart compulsively before culminating in a bout of anal incontinence so intense the Trickster is literally buried in a mountain of his own faeces, his actions are simultaneously amusing and appalling.

It's this peculiar human-yet-animal quality we see repeatedly echoed in mythologies around the world. For example, in *Signifying Animals: Human Meaning in the Natural World*, Olowo Ojoade recounts that in Nigerian folklore, animals initially lived together in a society separate from humans. However, when humans began to hunt and kill animals, the king of the humans and the king of the animals got together and made a deal: the humans would stop killing animals if given an animal to call their own. Votes were cast, and the dog was offered to the humans. Once in the human realm, dogs abandoned some of their crude ways and generally endeared themselves to humans. However, food shortages soon led the humans to hunt animals again, despite their treaty with the animal king, and the dogs proved adept at this as well. The animals blamed the dogs for this turn of events and pleaded with the humans to return canines to the animal kingdom, but the dogs, liking their new realm, refused to go. Animals and humans have been at loggerheads ever since.

But the similarities also have clear limits, given the tendency of dogs to engage in acts of incest* and faeces-consumption—activities that human societies generally find abhorrent. As Sigmund Freud observed in *Civilization and Its Discontents*, 'It would be incomprehensible, too, that man should use the name of his most faithful friend in the animal world—the dog—as a term of abuse if that creature had not incurred his contempt through two characteristics: that it is an animal... which has no horror of excrement, and that it is not ashamed of its sexual functions'. The anthropologist Edmund Leach similarly argued that this human-animal quality explains why dogs feature so frequently in insults hurled around the world. For example, the strongest way to insult one's enemies in Northern Thailand is to insinuate that a dog has had sexual intercourse with their ancestors.** While we are equal oppor-

---

*In stark contrast to humans and other primates, dogs make no distinction between kin and non-kin in mating preferences. This is a clear advantage for dog breeders, given that the exaggerated physical features of designer dogs can only be produced by high levels of inbreeding.

**Westerners are also quite fond of this insult. Witness the Albanian-hating scriptwriter played by Peter Falk in the film *Aunt Julia and*

tunists in the department of animal-inspired slurs (pig! cow! horse! cat! chicken!), there's little doubt that dogs are our preferred basis for insult—as put-downs like 'bitch', 'dog', 'mongrel', and 'cur'* attest.

This distinctiveness also manifests in the monikers dogs are generally bestowed in European and Anglophone countries. In the 1960s, the French anthropologist Claude Lévi-Strauss noted that dogs tend to be given names like those of humans but also different (such as Fido), while pet birds are given more typically human appellations (e.g., Polly). Lévi-Strauss argued that this is because dogs are more anatomically and socially connected to us than other pets. Birds, on the other hand, live in a parallel but separate society. Thus, a sort of cognitive disquiet occurs when we give dogs human names. Calling your pet bird 'Polly' is okay because they are clearly so much more different from us than dogs. But calling your dog 'George', especially if you know someone named George, well, that's asking for trouble.**

Although the lines between dog and human names have blurred to some degree over the past fifty-odd years, if lists of popular male and female dog names are anything to go by, there are still some subtle differences between them. While Rocky, Buddy, Zeus, Bandit, Samson, and

---

the Scriptwriter (based on Mario Vargas Llosa's book), whose favoured form of insult generally involved reference to the bestial sexual habits of Albanians—as in 'Sir, there's an Albanian outside and he's doing something unnatural to your German Shepherd'. I will have more to say about animal abuse in insults in 'You Can't Say "C*nt" in Canada'.

*Although this one seems to have been primarily relegated to bodice rippers.

**This explains why Madonna wasn't particularly flattered to find out that Graham Norton's dog was named after her.

Maximus are popular monikers for male dogs, few parents pick such names for their children—unless they want them to be teased mercilessly at school. Likewise, Lola, Angel, Princess, Ginger, Roxie, and Honey might be preferred appellations for female dogs, but this line-up of names is more likely to be found in a strip bar or drag club than your average school.*

The sense of outrage many Westerners express at the thought of eating dog** is also a testament to these human-animal qualities. As the anthropologist Marshall Sahlins observed in *Culture and Practical Reason*, the inedibility of dogs in North America has nothing to do with their intrinsic attributes (any more than our willingness to deem cattle 'food') and everything to do with the semi-human status we endow them with. In his words, dogs 'participate in American society in the capacity of subjects. They have proper personal names, and indeed we are in the habit of conversing with them as we do not talk to pigs and cattle'.*** Of course, it's precisely these qualities that explain

---

*That said, based on the number of women who have named their child Renesmee after reading Stephenie Meyer's *Twilight* series, we should never underestimate the willingness of parents to saddle their children with godawful names. My sister-in-law, a primary school teacher for more than thirty years in a regional Australian town, has numerous stories to tell of students with names like Handsome and Princess (siblings), Fish and Chips (another set of siblings), and Shithéad and Lemón (siblings again, although Lemón must be thanking his lucky stars at losing the 'Worst child's name ever' lottery).

**Often the same people horrified by dog-eaters don't blink an eye at eating cow or pig, two animals whose consumption produces equal horror amongst a substantial portion of the world's population.

***Anthropological insights on Americans' relationships with their dogs helped Mars to dramatically increase its market share in the pet food business. In *Anthro-Vision*, Gillian Tett discusses the research conducted by the consumer anthropologist Maryann McCabe for Mars on dog owners' relationships with their pets, which confirmed the semi-

why they tend to be eaten in the first place. When I was doing fieldwork in South Korea in the late 1990s and early 2000s, dog soup was consumed amongst various acquaintances, usually at the height of summer, primarily for its health-promoting properties. Likewise, Olowo Ojoade notes that dogs are occasionally eaten in Nigeria precisely because of their unique relationship with humans, which is perceived to imbue their flesh with magical properties. However, attitudes towards eating dog are changing in both countries—and others, such as China, appear to be following suit. This is partly due to Western condemnation of the practice as a 'cruel' and 'barbaric' tradition, but also because local sensibilities regarding dogs have shifted.

As the line between pets and food has hardened globally, the line between pets and humans has correspondingly softened—especially in relation to dogs. Peruse any pet shop, and the number of dog products vastly outweighs their feline counterparts, no doubt because of the different spending patterns of cat and dog owners. According to Statista, US dog owners spent twice as much on their pets as cat owners in 2020 and purchased almost three times as many gifts and splurge items. Family pooches are now commonly the recipient of birthday and Christmas presents, and the most successful pet influencers (yes, it's a thing) are canines, many with profiles their human counterparts would envy.* At the time of writing, the top

---

human status of dogs. This ultimately led Mars to change its marketing strategy away from a focus on animal health and science towards an emphasis on human relationships with dogs and anthropomorphized imagery of dogs themselves. It clearly worked; Tett notes that by 2020, Mars was earning more revenue by selling pet food than its eponymous chocolates.

*While there are some famous cat influencers, the most successful 'petfluencers' are dogs. Presumably, this is at least in part because most

dog, as it were, is JiffPom, a Pomeranian with more than thirty million followers on social media and a string of merchandise, movie deals, and music video appearances to his name.* However, perhaps the clearest illustration of the distinct ways dogs are being anthropomorphized is the growing popularity of 'neuticles'—prosthetic testicles for neutered pets. Although cats are equally fond of grooming their genitals, customer testimonials from their website suggest that the demand for fake balls stems exclusively from dog owners worried about damaging their pooch's self-esteem after the snip.**

As Donna Haraway has argued, we have always been intertwined with non-human animals. From dogs and cats to horses and cows, they have shaped us as much as we have shaped them over the course of our mutual histories. In her words, 'We are, constitutively, companion species'.

---

cats would refuse to cooperate—good luck dressing your cat in a tutu and getting it to prance about on two legs! It is telling that the most well-known cat influencer was nicknamed Grumpy Cat (RIP, Grumpy Cat), and not in an ironic way.

*JiffPom, who looks like an extremely photogenic cross between an Ewok and a teddy bear, is some sort of super-dog, with two Guinness World Records under his belt for being the fastest dog on two legs (he has the usual four but seems to have perfected the art of intermittent bipedalism). He can also shake hands, bow, and ride a skateboard and charges (or, rather, his owners charge) up to USD$32,045 for a single sponsored social media post.

**According to one happy Neuticles customer, 'He's a guy and I wanted him to remain looking like one'. It's difficult to imagine a cat owner purchasing a set of fake gonads for their pet feline on the same grounds. While this may well say something about the respective intelligence of cat and dog owners, I suspect it also speaks to the ways in which cats, regardless of their sex, have been culturally feminized (it's hardly a co-incidence that vaginas are nicknamed 'pussies'). As Ralph Bulmer has observed, his mother 'regards all dogs as male, and all cats as female', despite being broadly aware of the reproductive behaviour of these two species.

However, while the human-animal hierarchy we subscribe to may be an illusion, it's clear that dogs have a position of dubious privilege within it. Thus, the next time I suffer the indignity of a dog's unseemly interest in my crotch as it determines what manner of canine I am, I shall remind myself of the many indignities dogs suffer—bedazzled crotches and all—on the basis of our own unseemly interest in reproducing ourselves in our pets.

8

Menageries and Stock Markets

As an anthropologist relatively ignorant about the world of finance, it's nevertheless my impression that the terms 'bull' and 'bear' have gained much wider currency over the past fifteen years in explaining the state of the stock market. I recently made this observation to various family members who work in the investment sector and inquired about the origins of the terms. No one seemed to know, but the consensus was that 'bull' and 'bear' markets were purely descriptive phrases that have been used for centuries. If this was the case (and I was far from convinced it was), I argued that the terms as they are currently used are unlikely to mean the same thing as they did 150 years ago. Admittedly, I had no grounds for this claim beyond anthropological intuition that our perceptions of the stock market have changed over time.

My 'trust me, I'm an anthropologist' line went over about as well as you might expect, and—in the way of arguments everywhere—smartphones were pulled out to resolve the dispute. Soon my family were triumphantly brandishing quotes from 'authoritative' online sources, each of which seemed to attest to the lengthy history of the expressions. However, I remained sceptical. Are bulls and bears natural metaphors for the movements of the stock market? Why did these terms come to predominate, and when? Not one to lose an argument (or anything*) graciously, I decided to do some further digging into the topic.

Internet sources typically treat the terms 'bull' and 'bear' market as if their appropriateness to describe the stock market is intrinsic and self-explanatory. For example, Investopedia notes, in a somewhat patronizing tone, 'First of all, let's remember that bears are sluggish and bulls spirited and burly'—a characterization that anyone who has seen *The Revenant* would surely have cause to question.** Perhaps recognizing the facile nature of this explanation, various other origin stories frequently surface—ranging from the plausible to the wildly fanciful, with none standing up to scrutiny. For example, some commentators have suggested that the names are a logical reflection of the way bulls and bears attack: the bull thrusts its horns in the air, and the bear swipes down. However, this explanation only holds if you've never seen footage of an actual

*My sister has a scar on her lip from the ruthless tug-of-war over her iPad that occurred when we were playing a Scrabble game that I was winning and that she attempted to prematurely end. As the presence of the iPad suggests, we were well into adulthood when the fight occurred.

**When I lived in Canada, people would invariably comment on how dangerous Australian wildlife was. But wildlife attacks in Australia don't require you to make split-second assessments regarding the appropriate course of action based on your ability to discriminate the colour and size of said predator, ensuring certain death if you make the wrong call. Who, in the heat of the moment, can remember whether you're supposed to play dead for a grizzly or make yourself look big and threatening? Shouldn't there be some sort of memory aid for this scenario, which is surely more deserving of its own mnemonic than when to flush the toilet during water shortages (as in, 'if it's yellow let it mellow, if it's brown flush it down').

attack. For the record, you're more likely to be mauled by a bear's teeth than its claws, and anyone who thinks that bulls thrust their horns in the air to attack needs to watch the strikingly-literally-named YouTube video 'Actual footage of bull goring matador in butthole'.

Other explanations veer along apocryphal lines. For example, the *Morris Dictionary of Words and Phrase Origins* suggests that the most plausible theory for the terms is the old axiom about 'selling the skin before you've caught the bear', a practice allegedly employed by bearskin jobbers in eighteenth-century England. How this explains the 'bulls' part of the terminology isn't satisfactorily explained, although in *Bear Markets and Beyond: A Bestiary of Business Terms*, Dhruti Shah and Dominic Bailey suggest that the pairing stemmed from the blood sport of bull-and-bear fights.* Alternative theories speculate that the animal associations result from a terminological coincidence—namely, that in the early days of the London Stock Exchange, trading consisted primarily of a bulletin board on which traders could post offers to buy stock. When offers were abundant, the board was covered with bulletins, or 'bulls'.** When offers

---

*The problem is that this explanation is both apocryphal and anachronistic, given that the terms were introduced in the 1700s in England and bull-and-bear fights were a nineteenth-century American variation† on bull- and bear-baiting blood sports in Europe, both of which typically involved dogs.

†As far as I can tell, the American attitude to any imported sport is always 'Yes, but wouldn't it be better if...'—as in 'Wouldn't it be better if we developed a version of football that mostly involves picking up a ball and running with it', 'Wouldn't it be better if we developed a version of cricket with bigger dudes and smaller bats', 'Wouldn't it be better if instead of pitting bulls and bears against dogs, we pitted them against *each other*', etc. This is either a sign of American ingenuity at work or the desire to hold world championships for sports they always win.

**In some accounts, the board was 'full', which then morphed into 'bull' (clearly, in both senses of the word).

were scarce, the Exchange was 'bare' of offers.

The problem is that anyone can come up with a plausible-sounding story (or, for that matter, a patently ludicrous one) *after the fact*. To illustrate, here's one: 'bull' expresses the sorts of empty lies the market thrives on when it's going up; 'bear' alludes to what you have to do when the market is going down: grin and bear it. And here's another: 'bull' is short for bullion, which is a general reference to how rich investors get in a bull market; 'bear', sounding like its phonemic cousin 'beer', refers to the beverage that investors turn to in a market downturn as their champagne tastes must be satisfied on beer budgets. Although I just made these explanations up, are they any less credible than those we are typically presented with?

Unfortunately, my digging quickly revealed that the terms 'bull' and 'bear' have been used in relation to the stock market since at least the eighteenth century, but I was relieved to find that they didn't have meanings that directly equate to the way the terms are used today.* Take, for example, a book published by Thomas Mortimer in 1769 with one of those gloriously florid titles that eighteenth-century writers excelled in: *Every Man His Own Broker: Or, A Guide to Exchange-Alley in Which the Nature of Several Funds, Vulgarly Called the Stocks, is Clearly Explained and the Mystery and Inquity of Stock Jobbing Laid Before the Public in a New and Impartial Light*. In the book, Mortimer uses the terms 'bull' and 'bear' to characterize different types of investors, but his definitions hold little resemblance to their contemporary counterparts. In his words:

---

*Because otherwise you can rest assured that I would have pretended the argument never happened and avoided all further mention of the topic.

A Bull is the name by which the gentlemen of Exchange-Alley choose to call all persons who contract to
buy any quantity of government securities, without an
intention or ability to pay for it, and who consequently
are obliged to sell it again, either at a profit or a loss,
before the time comes, when they have contracted to
take it... In the interim he goes lowring* up and down
the house, and from office to office; and if he is asked a
civil question, he answers with a surly look, and by his
dejected, gloomy aspect and moroseness, he not badly
represents the animal he is named after.

A Bear, in the language of Exchange-Alley, is a person who has agreed to sell any quantity of the public
funds, more than he is possessed of, and often without
being possessed of any at all, which, nevertheless, he
is obliged to deliver against a certain time: before this
time arrives, he is continually going up and down seeking whom, or, which is the same thing, whole property
he can devour; you will find him in a continual hurry...
He is easily distinguished from the Bull, who is sulky
and heavy, and sits in some corner in a melancholy
posture; whereas the Bear, with meagre, haggard looks,
and a voracious fierceness in his countenance, is continually on the watch, seizes on all who enter the Alley.

The bulls and bears in Mortimer's account clearly
share some qualities with contemporary bullish and bearish investors in terms of their actions in purchasing and
selling stocks, but their traits were described in terms that
are virtually the opposite of how they are characterized today. For Mortimer, the bull was 'heavy', 'gloomy', 'morose',
and 'melancholy', while the bear was 'hurried', 'voracious',

---

*Lowring is an archaic spelling of lowering (rhymes with flowering)
and means to frown, scowl, look angry or sullen. It's rarely used today,
except by writers with literary pretensions, and mostly to describe an-
gry-looking clouds.

and 'fierce'. Thus, while the animal metaphors might not have changed, their associations unquestionably have.

These differences in how the bull/bear metaphors have been used over time tell us something important about the labels themselves: there is no straightforward connection between the nature of these animals and the movements of the stock market. Instead, they are better thought of as an instance of what anthropologists term 'totemic classification': a system in which the human and non-human world are conceptualized in relation to each other.

According to the French anthropologist Claude Lévi-Strauss, because of the function animals perform in totemic systems of classification, they can't be taken literally. Instead, they are a means of ordering and making sense of the world. Animals, he famously observed, are 'good to think' with. For example, in *The Savage Mind*, Lévi-Strauss discussed the ways in which the Iban of South Borneo derive omens by interpreting the song and flight of various species of birds. The cry of one type of bird is said to portend good hunting, a second augurs a successful trading expedition, and so on. In his words: 'It is obvious that the same characteristics could have been given a different meaning and that different characteristics of the same birds could have been chosen instead'. The point is not the nature of the signs themselves but how they relate to each other as part of a system.

Applying these insights to the notion of bull and bear investors, we can see that the animals aren't particularly important, despite the endless pontificating on their origins. Indeed, Mortimer's account suggests that the analogies would have worked just as well in reverse, so it seems an accident of history that today we talk about optimistic investors in terms of 'bulls' and their pessimistic counterparts in terms of 'bears'. Moreover, other animal analogies could easily have replaced them.

For example, if parents hadn't already claimed the terms as a euphemistic means of explaining the acts of reproduction and copulation to their bewildered children, there's no reason why we wouldn't now be talking about 'bird' and 'bee' investors instead.* The same goes for the use of 'doves' and 'hawks' to describe soft vs tough approaches to inflation and interest rates—although the terms were originally used in military circles, where the dove at least makes a degree of symbolic sense. In both instances, the value of the metaphors comes primarily from their utility as a way of conceptualizing and talking about difference; their meaning is thus *relational* rather than *intrinsic*.

But the thing with metaphors is that they often take on a life of their own. In their influential book *Metaphors We Live By*, George Lakoff and Mark Johnson assert that thought is fundamentally metaphoric in nature and that metaphors structure the way we think. Consider 'time is money'. As they note, we talk about wasting time, spending time, squandering time, investing time, budgeting time, living on borrowed time, using time, losing time, and so on. Although the metaphor is so taken for granted that we don't even realize we're using it, it reveals that we see time

---

*Birds and bees demonstrate the same totemic processes at work—they are hardly a natural metaphor for sexual intercourse and reproduction, as any child who has ever received the 'birds and the bees' talk will tell you. The origins of this expression are similarly obscure. For example, the *Morris Dictionary of Words and Phrase Origins* attributes the roots of the phrase to Samuel Taylor Coleridge's verse, 'The bees are stirring—birds are on the wing.' That might make sense if the terms were being used as a euphemism for sex in Coleridge's poem, but even some rather promising references to nectar and honey (staple euphemisms in romance novels for moist vaginas) turn out to be ponderous metaphors for the value of meaningful and industrious work.

Figure 8. *The Bulls and Bears in the Market*
by William Holbrook Beard, 1879

as a valuable commodity and a limited resource.* Thus, these kinds of key structuring metaphors aren't just *descriptive* but *productive*. Talk of 'losing' time bespeaks a particular orientation to time—for example, we stress about time in the same way we stress about money.

The same is true of the bull and bear metaphors, which have come to encompass not just investors but the market itself. Notice that in Mortimer's eighteenth-century account, the stock exchange wasn't described in totemic language—the terms were restricted to the humans who populated it. Today, however, we readily talk of 'bull' and

---

*The metaphor has been literalized in various dystopian sci-fi stories and films—like the Justin Timberlake turkey *In Time* and Harlan Ellison's short story '"Repent, Harlequin!" Said the Ticktockman'. Based on its thematic similarity to his book, Ellison sued the director of *In Time* for copyright infringement, insisting that he be listed in the credits—that is, until he actually saw the film, when he immediately dropped the lawsuit.

'bear' markets, although it's hard to pinpoint exactly when this happened.

For example, Robert Sobel's book *The Big Board: The History of the New York Stock Market*, published in 1965, is replete with references to bull and bear markets. The trouble is that it's mostly unclear whether the terms were widely used during the periods he was writing about. In other words, we might currently describe the stock market in the period leading up to the Great Depression as 'bearish', but is this a term—like the 'Great Depression' itself—that only came to be used later?* William Holbrook Beard's 1879 painting *The Bulls and Bears in the Market* (see figure 8) suggests the latter, depicting as it does the market as the site of a colossal brawl between bull and bear investors.

The change seems to have happened in the post-war period, although a 1977 paper by Frank Fabozzi and Jack Francis in the *Journal of Finance* suggests some debate about the intensity and duration required for a market trend to be characterized as 'bullish' or 'bearish'. But another shift occurred towards the end of the twentieth century when the terms became popularized outside the financial sector. At this point, they were no longer used as straightforward descriptors of upward and downward market movements but came to describe broader market mentalities. For example, a 2001 piece in *The Times* by Mark Atherton titled 'Market mumbo jumbo explained' begins: 'With stock markets around the globe turning nervous in the past couple of weeks, investors are probably suffering from an overdose of

---

*Likewise, the First World War obviously wasn't called that at the time, which would have been a sign of spectacularly bad faith on the part of its combatants. In contrast to the Great Depression, which posthumously got its name from the British economic historian Lionel Robbins, the First World War was contemporaneously known as the 'Great War'—no one was expecting an even more lethal repeat twenty-one years later.

financial jargon'. Notice that it's not the investors that are 'turning nervous' but the stock market itself. This might seem an insignificant distinction, but it's a perfect example of what Karl Marx termed 'commodity fetishism': when capital is spoken of in terms usually reserved for people and animate beings. The result is that money and the stock market seem to take on a life of their own. Money appears unnaturally fertile (it 'grows'), and the market becomes a living, breathing organism seemingly separable from investors themselves.

In her book *Anthro-Vision*, Gillian Tett, an anthropologist and the editor-at-large of the *Financial Times*, has discussed how the insularity of the world of banking created a situation in which bankers misread the signs of the imminent global financial crisis in the lead-up to 2008. Describing her experiences at an investment banking conference in 2005, she highlights the striking absence of humans in financiers' presentations on debt, liquidity, and the market. 'Who is borrowing this money? Where are the humans? How does this connect to real life?', she asked herself. It was only those few financial experts who shifted their attention from spreadsheets and screens to the people who inhabited the housing market that were able to see the signs of impending collapse. As the narrator notes in the opening scene of the film *The Big Short*,* which immortalizes those who accurately predicted the financial crisis, 'These outsiders saw the giant lie at the heart of the economy, and they saw it by doing something the rest of the suckers never thought to do: they looked'. Meeting a

*The movie is based on the 2010 book *The Big Short: Inside the Doomsday Machine* by Michael Lewis. Various names have been changed in the film version and a degree of artistic license has been taken. For example, the scene at the Florida strip club in the film is recounted as an anecdote in the book about a Las Vegas stripper with five mortgages.

Florida stripper with mortgages on five houses and a con-do, brokers hitting their bonus targets by offering NINJA* mortgage loans, and so on revealed the housing market as a house of cards.**

According to Tett, the experience of seeing the 'living, breathing humans' within the financial chain showed the contradictions in the system. But one of the reasons so few financial experts bothered to look at the actual humans involved in the market was that they were too busy looking at the market *itself* as a living, breathing entity. After all, for the stock market to take on a life of its own, the social relationships underpinning it must be concealed so that it effectively appears to produce itself. Indeed, the business scholar Michael Morris and his colleagues have demon-strated that using agent metaphors like 'bull' and 'bear' to describe the stock market, with their implication of price movements as 'the volitional, internally-driven behavior of an animate entity', have a direct impact on people's expec-tations of market trend continuance.

This is why financial experts repeatedly warn of the dangers of anthropomorphizing the stock market—'Stop thinking about markets as if they were human: your port-folio will do better if you do', a Bloomberg article declares. Likewise, in *Fooled by Randomness: The Hidden Role of Chance in Life and Markets*, Nassim Nicholas Taleb argues that the terms 'bullish' and 'bearish' are used by people who refuse to recognize market uncertainty. However, this implies that anthropomorphizing the stock market is an aberration

*They were not giving loans to actual ninjas; it's an acronym for 'no income, no job'.

**Actually, Jenga is the preferred analogy in the film. I, for one, am all for jettisoning the 'house of cards' expression, which I think we can all agree makes much less sense now than in 1645, when building houses out of cards was an actual pastime.

rather than intrinsic to its operation.

In his 1936 book, *The General Theory of Employment, Interest, and Money*, the influential economist John Maynard Keynes suggested that 'animal spirits' were critical to capitalism. According to Keynes, capitalism wasn't driven by reasonable calculation alone; instead, it required animal spirits that provided the kind of spontaneous optimism that encouraged investment. For Keynes, in a market based purely on mathematical expectation, 'enterprise will fade and die'. However, Keynes noted that the animal spirits of capitalism also had their downside. With so much riding on sentiment, slumps and depressions became exaggerated in degree. Of course, the point holds even truer now, as the world of screens and computers has replaced the physical interactions upon which the stock market used to depend. In this environment, it's difficult to remember that market volatility is merely a reflection of investor sentiment, and it starts looking like the cause rather than the effect— ironically increasing said volatility as investors scramble to respond to 'the market'. In this context, the stock market really does appear to produce itself.

So what did I discover from my excursion into the world of financial bestiaries? Most importantly, I learnt that I was right (well, mostly). While the terms 'bull' and 'bear' have been used for centuries in relation to the stock market, they aren't innocent descriptors but instead speak to the human tendency to think totemically: to understand the human world in relation to the natural one. The metaphors also expanded and mutated as we nurtured them— just like the adorable creature in the 1980s classic *Gremlins* that transforms into a horde of psychotic monsters when fed and watered. However, if the stock market has become a monster, it's more like a golem than a gremlin. A being created from inanimate matter that has been magically brought to life through incantations and spells, in Jewish mythology the golem is dangerous but not evil, although without due care it can escape the control of its masters and run amok. This seems a far more apt metaphor for the stock market than the prevailing animal spirits; as a bonus, it would also make for some rather eye-catching statues on Wall Street!

9

The Illogic of Tipping

As an Australian, tipping rules are not intuitive,*
although I've lived for almost twenty years in countries where gratuities are common. I clearly recall one incident that occurred more than a decade after moving to
Canada. The specific occasion was the steam cleaning of
my carpet.** The cleaners had been hard at work for almost an hour and were starting to wrap things up when
I was suddenly struck by a disturbing thought: was I sup-

*According to the anthropologist John Frank Burgess, tipping was
introduced in Australia in the late nineteenth century—the same time
it made an appearance in the USA. However, it didn't take off, in part
because of different kinds of labour relations between employers and
employees, but also because the practice of tipping became associated
with American culture and therefore a perceived threat to the Australian way of life. However, tipping has become increasingly common
in Australia, although it remains largely confined to capital cities like
Sydney. Australians typically treat this as proof that they were right to
be afraid of Americanization and many have taken to Twitter to express
their rage. Angry diatribes can also readily be found on TripAdvisor advising tourists that the minimum wage in Australia is $20.33 per hour
and wait staff don't require tips to survive.

**Er, that's not a euphemism for anything. I was literally having my
carpets cleaned.

posed to give them a tip? The thing is that despite being a social anthropologist, I have not reliably been able to determine when I should provide a tip—although living in countries with different norms around tipping hasn't helped my confusion.

Two years after arriving in Canada, I discovered that people generally tip hairdressers. Miraculously, my hairdresser, who I ultimately had for a decade, didn't hold this against me.* In my experience, British hairdressers don't expect tips in the same way as their North American counterparts. The few times I've tried to tip hairdressers in London have been disastrous—one seemed embarrassed and the other informed me dismissively that she only accepted cash tips, and I wasn't carrying any money. Indeed, a 2020 YouGov survey suggests that Brits are split on whether hairdressers and barbers should be tipped: 29% of respondents indicated that they always tip, and 24% indicated that they never do. The only context where British people seem to consistently tip on service is at restaurants—although the tip is often built into the bill as a 'discretionary service charge'.** The YouGov survey suggests that Brits are relatively divided on whether taxi drivers should be tipped,

---

*I didn't learn this while living in the USA, because I never went to the hairdresser—this being the phase of life when I refused to pay for such things as haircuts and dentists. It was only after we moved to Canada that I started going to the hairdresser regularly—my sister insisted upon it after one of my DIY haircuts left me with an extremely noticeable bald patch that I had to cover with brown eyeshadow until my hair grew back out.

**Interestingly, almost half of respondents indicated that they had asked for a service charge to be removed at least once in the past and 10% indicated that they always demand this. North American tourists, on the other hand, are wont to double-tip. Not being used to the service charge being included on the bill, they often add an extra tip, which goes to show that you should *always* read your bill.

and virtually no one tips delivery drivers, bar staff, or at fast-food outlets.

The situation is rather different in North America, where tipping is much more widespread. In Canada, people generally leave coins in a tip jar when ordering at cafés without table service, and electronic payment systems often include a tip as a default option. Indeed, I was publicly called out in Montréal for not tipping at a takeaway outlet. While waiting for our order, in response to an Australian colleague's query about whether she should leave a tip, I responded authoritatively, 'Nah, only when you get table service.' The cashier overheard my response and loudly corrected me. I can't remember all the details of the unsolicited excursion into Quebec's tax laws that followed, but the gist was that tipping was factored into food servers' wages, so they were taxed for it whether they received the additional income or not. Outwardly humbled, we both gave a generous tip and slinked out of the shop.* This incident left me more bewildered than ever about tipping practices. How is tipping someone who literally just brings me my order different from the service provided by a store cashier or sales assistant, none of whom seemed to expect any sort of tip for their efforts—even the friendly woman at the local supermarket who packed groceries like a Tetris Master.

If I'm being honest, there have been various occasions when I have not tipped. One time, after receiving appallingly bad service at a Vancouver restaurant, I wrote on the receipt 'please turn over for tip', and then proceeded to detail on the back of it precisely what they could have done

---

*I mean, I continued not to tip when I got takeaway in Canada, but I tried to be less obvious about it.

to receive an actual tip.* On another occasion at a Whistler café, I tried to explain to the server why I wasn't leaving a tip. This, I thought, would be less cowardly than just not tipping. Plus, I didn't want her to assume that I had *accidentally* failed to leave a tip because I was Australian;** I wanted her to know that I had *intentionally* failed to leave a tip because of the terrible service. This extremely awkward exchange took place in front of my husband and his brother, who happened to be visiting from Australia, as well as, obviously, the café at large. Even my brother-in-law could see that I was committing a major faux pas. Both rushed out of the café, pretending they didn't know me.

While my lack of formative experience with tipping partly explains my confusion, it's clear that many people find it a social minefield—at least according to the You-Gov survey. Even in the USA, where tipping is ubiquitous, people still find the practice anxiety-producing. As the historian Kerry Segrave notes in *Tipping: An American Social History of Gratuities*, 'Many people are uncomfortable in tipping situations; they are unsure of whom to tip and how much'.*** Part of the reason why tipping creates wide-

---

*In my defence, the idea came from a series of Australian Pizza Hut ads in the 1990s that played on the preposterousness of tips to Australian eyes. Featuring Dougie the pizza boy, in various commercials he optimistically asks for a tip when out delivering pizzas and gets treated to bits of wisdom like 'Always put your park break on when you park your van' and 'Work hard and be good to your mother'.

**Australians have a reputation (not undeserved, it must be said) for being terrible tippers. I recall on various occasions in Canada being treated to a look of resignation when taxi drivers heard my accent, and then surprised delight if I provided a decent tip. One taxi driver captured the general sentiment when he exclaimed, upon receipt of a good tip, 'But you're Australian! You lot are the *worst* tippers.'

***This uncertainty is manifested in the endless (mostly inaccurate) guides to tipping customs, which seem to primarily be written by and

spread confusion is its intrinsically ambiguous nature. In *The Social Meaning of Money*, the sociologist Viviana Zelizer captures this quality perfectly, observing that tipping has always presented a fundamental puzzle because it lies at the boundaries of other kinds of transfers: 'not quite a payment, not quite a bribe, not quite charity, but not quite a gift either'.

The standard explanation for tipping is that its motivations are primarily economic. As the social psychologist Boas Shamir observes, we generally treat the tip as a payment for something 'extra' in situations where the commodity being sold contains non-standardized components—namely, a service instead of (or as well as) a good. However, this view of tipping fits poorly with the reality of the practice. To quote the anthropologist George Foster's blunt assessment, these explanations of tipping are 'pure folklore, totally unrelated to fact'. If the motivations for tipping were purely economic, then the tip would reflect the amount of effort invested by the service giver. But tip percentages are typically standardized,* and tip size is often determined by factors that have nothing to do with

---

for Americans. Interestingly, these guides often focus on explaining how to tip in countries where the practice is neither common nor desired. For example, *Condé Naste Traveler's* 'Etiquette 101: Your guide tipping around the world' advises that travellers in Australia and New Zealand should tip waiters, concierges, housekeepers, guides, and drivers, but 'Be discreet and prepare to have your tip refused, especially in New Zealand, where people are particularly reserved'. Here's a thought: just advise people not to tip!

*For example, when I lived in Vancouver, it was considered standard to tip 15% at restaurants. The rise of digital payments has exacerbated tip inflation because the default settings for tips generally start at 18%—many places in Vancouver now have a 30% tip option! Moreover, tips are always set on the post-tax amount. Canadians don't seem to have a problem with this, but every Australian expat I knew in Canada objected to this because 'you don't tip on tax'.

the quality of the service offered—unless one considers the breast size* or hair colour of their server integral to the experience of eating a meal. The fact is that while customers are theoretically free to skip the tip, from the most rudimentary (and rude) service to the most obsequious and over-the-top, North American wait staff, taxi drivers, and so on *expect* gratuities.**

Challenging the economic argument even further is the form the payment should take. Before electronic payments became common, it was considered demeaning or insulting to use pennies in a tip, even if the tip itself was for a standard amount. As the anthropologist Leo Pap has pointed out, gratuities are also supposed to be round amounts—as in $2, not $1.99. All this would suggest that any analysis of tipping must consider social and cultural

---

*In a finding that will surprise absolutely no one, a survey by the American psychologist Michael Lynn found that waitresses in their thirties, those with large breasts, blonde hair and/or slender bodies received larger tips than those without these characteristics. The Hooters chain of sports bars, or, as *The Sun*† calls them, 'breastaurants', was basically founded on this premise. In 2021, Hooters changed their waitresses' uniforms to include shorts (a term I use loosely) that wouldn't look out of place on a Brazilian beach. Although initially insistent that staff who refused to wear the pants would either have to change to a non-image-based position or resign, the head office eventually made the shorts optional after the public outcry. Interestingly, several waitresses have stated their preference for the new shorts because they make 'way more money' in tips.

†Given that *The Sun's* business model operates on the same premise (they pioneered the Page Three girl and pictures of scantily clad celebrities are still their bread and butter), I suspect that they only reported on the Hooters' uniform controversy because it gave them an excuse to plaster pictures of waitresses clad in booty shorts all over the article.

**When I was in New York a few years back, I was told by one taxi driver that the 10% tip I had given him wasn't large enough and 20% was standard. However, as he only accepted cash payments, he was forced (bitterly, it must be said) to accept my 'measly' tip.

factors as well as economic ones. To quote Shamir: 'The tip, like the gift, is given under voluntary guise, but in fact under a constraining normative framework in situations where the mutual obligations are not exactly specified'.*

Numerous scholars have observed that tipping is most prominent where a menial personal service is offered. After all, gratuities are expected by waiters but not chefs, and cab drivers but not mechanics. According to Leo Pap, 'If one common denominator can be found for the large majority of tippee categories it seems to be this: Tip-dependent workers render relatively unskilled personal services historically associated with what a private host's servants do for his guests—more specifically those categories of private servants that are in direct face-to-face contact with guests'. As the 1933 *Oxford English Dictionary* defined it, a tip is 'a small present of money given to an inferior, especially to a servant or employee of another for a service rendered or expected'. Indeed, Kerry Segrave suggests that tipping has its origins in the practice of 'vails', which became commonplace during the Tudor period, and involved visitors to private homes giving sums of money at the end of their stay for the additional services rendered by their host's servants to accommodate guests. As it became increasingly common for the gentry to stay in commercial establishments, this practice evolved and 'vails' became 'tips' somewhere along the way.**

---

*Although we tend to think of gifts as one-off expressions of altruism and generosity, the French sociologist Marcel Mauss decisively shattered the idea of the unfettered gift with no strings attached. I will have more to say on the gift in 'Beware of Colleagues Bearing Drinks'.

**One apocryphal tale is that the latter term stems from the practice of a London coffee house to place a bowl on tables carrying the words 'To Insure Promptitude', or 'TIP' for short. This strikes me as a questionable post-hoc justification, or, to put it in plain English, bullshit.

According to Pap, the association of tipping with menial personal service explains why some people are offended at being offered a tip. Indeed, the more important a service is, the less likely it is to be a tipped profession. It's not appropriate to tip your dentist, your mechanic, or your child's teacher, although it would be acceptable to offer another kind of gift-in-kind, such as chocolates, etc. This, Pap suggests, is because of the different connotations of non-monetary gifts vs 'naked money', although it's also presumably because tipping in these contexts readily slides into something else entirely. It might be charitable to tip your waiter, but it's illegal to tip your local teacher—try it and you may find yourself up on bribery charges.* And if a police officer expects a tip to give you better service, well, there's a label for that too ('extortion').

Based on the status differences between the actors involved, some scholars have suggested that tipping is about establishing the dominance and superiority of the tipper over the service provider. According to Boas Shamir, 'The gratuity from this perspective is not an expression of gratitude, as is commonly believed, but rather a defense against gratitude... Its aim is not so much to motivate the service-giver as to confirm the superior status of the customer, in a way which does not allow any reciprocal "correction"'. Conversely, the anthropologist George Foster has argued that tipping is less a means of asserting superiority over those in servile positions and more a symbolic device intended to neutralize envy by giving them a token payment.**

---

*It's probably worth noting that in various parts of the Middle East and South Asia, tipping, charitable giving, and political bribes are known by the same word.

**Foster suggests that the token payment is proportionate to the value of a snack or a drink. He thus endorses the theory that the term 'tip' is

Not entirely convinced by either argument, Shamir suggests that tipping is best conceptualized as a response to the impersonal nature of the market economy because it gives a sense of control in interactions where it's otherwise lacking. In his words, 'By giving something to the other side, above and beyond the agreed upon price, the buyer or seller may demonstrate, to himself as well as others, that he is not fully trapped in the non-individual, unhuman market mechanism, and that he has retained some capability for voluntary non-profitable action'. In this framing, tipping is a means of asserting individualism, which may explain why the practice has been so widely embraced in the USA.

Despite being the country most associated with gratuities, tipping in its modern American form is a surprisingly recent development: more of a suspect interloper than a revered ancestor. According to Segrave, European travel writers and visitors travelling to the USA in the nineteenth century frequently expressed their amazement that they were not expected to tip. Indeed, the practice had strongly European connotations for both the working-class Americans introduced to tipping by European migrants and the wealthy Americans who brought the custom back from their European travels as a sign of their continental sophistication.

Partly due to these associations, there was immense resistance when tipping was first introduced. It was only in the early twentieth century that the practice became commonplace in the USA—in the face of not-inconsiderable opposition. While some approved of tipping as facilitating

---

etymologically related to 'tipple', given that the term for 'tip' in many languages has associations with drinking—for example, *pourboire* in French (literally 'to drink'), *trinkgeld* in German ('drink money'), and *propina* in Spanish ('to give a drink to, to treat').

fraternity and goodwill, others saw it as a crass corruption of the gift. For example, the sternly named 'Society for the Prevention of Useless Giving' pointed to the moral and social evils of gratuities.

William Scott's *The Itching Palm: A Study of the Habit of Tipping in America*, published in 1916, recounted the major criticisms. 'Tipping is the modern form of Flunkyism', he railed. Denouncing it as un-American, Scott characterized tipping as an aristocratic custom designed to instil a sense of servitude. For Scott, tipping engendered a grafting spirit ('the Barbary pirates would have been ashamed to go it that strong!'), rigidified class distinctions, and encouraged a loss of self-respect. It was, in his words, 'what we left Europe to escape. It is a cancer in the breast of democracy'.

As a result of such sentiments, there were various attempts to abolish tipping by turning it into a punishable misdemeanour. According to the labour historian Dorothy Cobble, between 1909 and 1918, seven US states enacted anti-tipping laws. Union activists and female social reformers also condemned the habit as reinforcing low wages and encouraging immorality in waitresses dependent on male customers for their livelihood. Union officials observed that tipping created a dynamic that made it difficult for waitresses to 'draw where the line of propriety should be' because without it, most wouldn't have made enough money to live on. Indeed, Cobble observes that as a result of tipping, the financial potential of waitressing often exceeded that of other more skilled professions open to women. Nevertheless, this potential was rarely realized—at least in the long term. After all, decent tips generally correlated with the woman's possession of youthful good looks: as she got older, the tips got smaller.

In light of this history, it's somewhat surprising that tips have become such an integral part of the US economy that the minimum cash rate for tipped professions is $2.13 per hour, based on the assumption that the bulk of their wages will be paid by customers themselves. In other words, public goodwill has effectively been institutionalized in the US wage system. Yet, some of those most ardently opposed to scrapping the practice and bringing the minimum wage for tipped professions up to the national standard are tipped workers themselves. This is primarily because of the promise of earning more than the standard minimum wage, which at $7.25 per hour clearly isn't enough to actually live on. This promise might not be realized, at least consistently, but it dangles alluringly in the distance—like the idea of an exciting and memorable New Year's Eve.*

In effect, tipping appears to have been inflected with a sort of quintessentially American logic. For the tippers, it creates a sense of individual control over an impersonal market interaction. For the tippees, it seems to be perpetuated by the belief that if you're good enough, determined enough, and work hard enough, you can rise above your circumstances. The problem is that, like the American Dream, it seems to legitimize—and thrive on—inequality: wage inequality between tipped and non-tipped professions, and between those individuals whose physical attributes facilitate good tips and those who don't. As Scott observed in 1916: 'if the $200,000,000 or more annually [the figure is well over $42 billion now] given to those serving the public should be withdrawn suddenly, employers would face the necessity of a radical readjustment of wage

*It's a well-known fact that New Year's Eve is the most overrated day of the year. *The Washington Post* insists that there is now scientific proof of this, because a US study found that 83% of respondents were disappointed by their NYE celebration. (I can only assume that the other 17% were too drunk or stoned to remember their evening.)

systems'—a readjustment that would, of necessity, expand to include non-tipped as well as tipped professions.

Despite its repressive effects on the minimum wage, tipping is now so entrenched in North America that it's difficult to see how change might occur, although various restaurants in New York have instigated 'no tipping' policies and raised wages and menu prices accordingly. Yes, that's right, without tipping, menu prices are invariably higher, which partly explains why some North Americans categorically reject the concept. But unless you're a stingy tipper, it wouldn't necessarily change the overall bill. Plus, you get to experience the novel pleasure of knowing at the start of the meal exactly how much it will cost. However, this would mean relinquishing the myth that tipping improves service and that the payment is purely economic—a view that has proved difficult to eradicate, despite all the evidence to the contrary.

Over a hundred years ago, when Scott penned his diatribe on tipping, he declared, 'Some day this majority will rise up and deal as summarily with the tipping practices as our forefathers dealt with the Mediterranean tribute custom!' Sadly, this prediction has so far proved to be wildly optimistic, especially as the practice has spread around the globe. However, if the demise of tipping occurs, it will likely be technology that kills it. The rise of digital payments is clearly changing the nature of tipping, as servers can no longer rely on immediate cash tips, and employers are more liable to assert ownership over tip-generated income. In effect, the flexible and evasive character that historically characterized tipping is now disappearing, and technology is serving to erase the personal and individualized aspects of the practice that made it attractive in the first place. So I live in the hope that US proposals to increase the minimum wage will expand to include tipped professions as well. While tipping might not be a 'cancer in the breast of democracy', it's at the very least a boil on its arse—and the time has surely come to lance the wound.

10

Beware of Colleagues Bearing Drinks

Shortly after moving to Colorado, I was introduced to the Friday Afternoon Club: a social event at the university where I worked. Consisting of faculty from various academic departments, it involved meeting up at a local brewery from about 4 p.m. each Friday afternoon to usher in the weekend. However, a month or so into my job, I gave up on the FAC, concluding that the faculty who attended were a bunch of tight arses. This unattractive frugality in my fellow club members had been starkly apparent from the first time I attended the FAC. After settling into a corner booth, I offered to 'shout' everyone a drink—a standard ploy for the first-time entrant to any established drinking circle in my native Australia. No one understood the term, and requests for clarification followed. Slightly stumped on the best way to explain it, I responded that a 'shout' was essentially the same as a 'treat'—I would 'treat' them all to a drink. Everyone looked surprised but hesitantly assented, and I bought them a round of drinks.

When we had finished our beers, the server came to take our order and I looked expectantly at my fellow faculty members—one of whom would now presumably buy a second round. My expectations were quickly shattered when everyone individually ordered a second beer. Feeling slightly chagrined, I had a second drink and then left. This phenomenon reoccurred, with little variation, the following week. I volunteered to treat everyone to a drink, people demurred, I insisted, they looked uncomfortable, and there was some exchanging of glances (and rolling of eyes), but no one offered to buy a second round. At that point, I concluded that this lot were never going to take the hint and stopped attending regularly. It was only much later that I was struck by the realization that the term 'treat' is a very poor substitution for 'shout'.* In reflecting on the differences between them, it dawned on me that I may have been a little hasty in dismissing my co-workers as 'scabby** bastards who wouldn't fork out a dollar if their lives depended on it' based on a cultural mistranslation of the word 'shout'.

For those unfamiliar with the term, the Australian shout shares much in common with the practice of buying rounds in the UK and elsewhere. It involves everyone in a party taking turns to buy drinks; once a shout is initiated, it's theoretically not complete until everyone in the party has had their turn. The rules of shouting are explicitly about reciprocity. I buy you a drink and then comes the most important bit: *you buy me one.* A 'treat', on the other hand, is provided at the expense of the giver, ostensibly

---

*This realization occurred when I was in the middle of giving a lecture on anthropological conceptions of the gift. As this book reveals, anthropologists are often spectacularly bad at applying the concepts they traffic in professionally to their own lives.

**'Scab' or 'scabby' in Australian English is the direct equivalent of 'tight arse' or 'tight' in British English and 'penny pincher' in American English and means 'to obtain goods by imposing on another's generosity'.

as an expression of their personal regard and generosity of spirit. Thus, telling someone that you will 'treat' them is an indication that you will pick up the tab without any expectation of reciprocity, which was precisely the opposite of the meaning I intended to convey.

But this wasn't merely a case of using the wrong terminology to describe an action known by a different name in the USA.* There simply isn't a culturally institutionalized practice equivalent to 'shouting' or 'round buying' in its Australian and British senses. Indeed, the concept of 'buying rounds' in the USA has entirely different connotations, given that a Google search on the term brings up information about gun and ammunition sales.** The closest equivalent is the idea of buying a round of drinks for the entire bar.*** An *Esquire* article by Ross McCammon on the etiquette of the practice characterizes it as an act of spontaneous generosity that someone might choose to undertake because: 'you're having a kid', 'you've inherited a great sum of money and enough time has passed that

*For example, 'root', 'shag', and 'bang' are Australian, British, and American slang terms and direct synonyms: all denote the act of having sex in a casual and indiscriminate sort of fashion. Incidentally, this is the reason why Australians find the Canadian clothing brand 'Roots' hilarious (especially their 'Roots Kids' t-shirts), along with the American plumbing company 'Mr. Rooter', and his promise to 'clean out your pipes'.

**This is probably as good an illustration as any regarding the differences between American, Australian, and British culture.

***The American preference for the term 'bar' over 'pub' or 'tavern' is telling. In Australia and England, 'bar' has distinctly American connotations. On his *Zythophile* blog, Martyn Cornell posits that English pubs have regulars and bars have customers, because the former is a place for socializing (a 'public house') whereas the latter is effectively a shop that sells drinks. I don't think the conceptual distinction holds in the same way in the USA, but it's interesting that the preferred term emphasizes the transactional rather than social aspect of drinking.

you are no longer grieving', 'you won the lottery', or 'the diagnosis was incorrect'.

The problem is that anthropologists have long cast doubt on the existence of spontaneous generosity. As James Carrier observes, far from being unprompted expressions of sentiment, gifts in industrial capitalist societies tend to be 'recurrent, predictable and socially regulated'. In his classic 1925 work *The Gift*, the famed French sociologist Marcel Mauss showed that the idea of the pure, unfettered gift is a fallacy. According to Mauss, societies are characterized by two distinct types of exchange: commodity exchange and gift exchange. Market economies are based on commodity exchange. In this context, self-interested, independent individuals engage in transactions with people with whom they have no enduring links or obligations. Objects are defined exclusively by the uses to which they may be put or what they may be exchanged for, which is generally money. As I discussed in 'Menageries and Stock Markets', market exchange systems enable goods to be removed from the social relations involved in their production, which is why we tend to think of the stock market as an independent, sentient entity. But in systems based on gift exchange, objects are connected with the identities of those who exchange them. The objects exchanged bind the giver and the recipient in a web of social obligations: obligations to give, receive, and reciprocate.

Although Mauss treated gift and commodity exchange as distinct cultural forms, anthropologists inspired by his work saw them as different kinds of relations that potentially existed within the same society. After all, while market-based economies involve the circulation of commodities, they also involve the circulation of gifts. We exchange gifts all the time—including formal presents, along with a variety of informal favours, services, and activities. For example, helping a friend move house is a gift; so is watering your neighbours' plants when they go away. As the anthropologist Gillian Tett notes, 'if you take a wider lens, you can see that we are surrounded by all manner of exchanges that do not carry monetary tags or end in a neat bounded manner, as economic models might imply'. Problems arise when we fail to recognize that these gifts operate by the core principle that Mauss identified: namely, the requirement for reciprocity. This is one of the reasons why tipping causes so much confusion—because it's effectively caught between these two different types of exchange; the same is also true of bonuses.* And, of course, denying the principle of reciprocity causes acute problems in the context of presents and other non-monetary favours. To quote Mary Douglas, 'By ignoring the universal custom of compulsory gifts we make our own record incomprehensible to ourselves'.

Most people instinctively know that gifts generally come with strings attached, leaving the recipient beholden to the giver.** This ambivalence is evident in expressions such as 'Beware of Greeks bearing gifts' and 'Never look a gift horse in the mouth'. While the former warns against trusting the motives of an adversary who shows unexpected

---

*Bonuses are often ideologically framed as gifts but they are generally expected and may even be written into employees' contracts—in this respect, they operate in the manner of tips. Moreover, even when bonuses aren't laid out formally and explicitly linked to performance, employees have a clear sense of what they are 'owed' and often whinge if their bonus isn't high enough. It's only when the amount is higher than expected that it's perceived as a gift rather than an entitlement.

**This is evident in the history of the term 'treat' itself, which initially meant to negotiate or bargain with, and came to mean entertaining someone with food or drink, sometimes in the manner of a bribe. In this context, the treat is part of a social exchange—either a reward for actions or favours, or an inducement for such.

generosity, and the latter warns against a mercenary attitude towards gifts, both suggest the complex motivations involved in giving and receiving. This is why we're often wary when we receive a spontaneous gift from someone we don't know well, why the question of who pays for dinner on a first date can be fraught, and why we start feeling resentful when friends constantly ask for favours but never return them. As the anthropologist Marshall Sahlins observed, gifts reflect social relationships: the closer the relationship, the less explicit the requirement for reciprocity tends to be.

Looking after your grandkids and giving your siblings hand-me-down clothes, cars, or furniture are examples of generalized reciprocity. Sahlins characterizes these kinds of transactions as 'putatively altruistic' because the material side of the transaction is repressed by the social side, and there is no explicit reckoning of debts. But make no mistake: reciprocal obligations *are* incurred; it's just that they are oblique rather than direct and aren't stipulated by time, quantity, or quality.* Balanced reciprocity, on the other hand, is typical when the relationship is less personal and the parties involved confront each other as distinct economic and social interests. It takes the form of a direct exchange—a 'like-for-like' scenario. According to Sahlins, in this type of exchange, 'the reciprocation is the customary equivalent of the thing received and is without delay', like buying rounds at a pub. But things go awry when the type of exchange doesn't match the social relationship—for example, grandparents demanding cash or a favour every time they look after your kids, or the guy you

---

*So if you think that your parents are babysitting your kids every week purely because they love spending time with your little angels, expect to learn otherwise when you inform them that you're skipping the family Christmas to go on a Caribbean holiday instead.

meet through Tinder insisting on buying you an expensive meal on your first date,* or your new Australian colleague offering to 'treat' everyone to a drink.

Recall that my co-workers were distinctly uncomfortable with my offer to buy them a beer, and their discomfort noticeably intensified the second time around. In McCammon's article on how to buy a round of drinks for everyone in the bar, he similarly notes that sober people are likely to be bemused by the act, asking, 'Who is this guy?' Ostentatious acts of altruism by relative strangers are generally perceived as status displays:** an attempt by the giver to place themselves above the recipient. Certainly, most of us have witnessed status-oriented displays of generosity of this kind—a phenomenon captured in David Sedaris's short story 'Christmas Means Giving'. In the story, a game of one-upmanship between a couple and their new next-door neighbours rapidly devolves into acts of competitive gift-giving, with each couple trying to outdo the other with increasingly outlandish acts of generosity. The narrator and his wife give away their house, money, and children. He also donates his internal organs and eyes, and his wife removes her teeth, scalp, right leg, and both breasts before realizing they're not transplantable. As the narrator notes, 'If practiced correctly, generosity can induce feelings of shame, inadequacy, and even envy'.

The impact of gift-giving on social relations is critical to understanding the presence of the shout in Australia

---

*He might want your regard, but he definitely wants a root.

**Indeed, McCammon implies that this is basically what buying a round for the bar is, because he advises that it's best to display your generosity in a public way, screaming at the top of your lungs, 'next round's on me!', rather than leaving cash with the bartender on the way out and telling him to use it to buy everyone drinks.

and its relative absence in the USA.* The anthropologist Bruce Kapferer has discussed at length the cultural value Australians place on egalitarian individualism: a kind of group-oriented individualism that downplays artificial differences. He suggests that this manifests in the cultural emphasis on 'mateship' and its refusal of status distinctions. People who set themselves above others based on wealth, influence, or education are colloquially known as 'tall poppies' and quickly cut down to size.** Indeed, a culturally sanctioned contempt for social hierarchy has long marked Australian national identity, which explicitly

---

*It's also key to understanding round buying in England. In *Watching the English*, Kate Fox suggests that English pubs are socially integrative, egalitarian environments that bring together people of different ages, social classes, education levels, and occupations. The primary difference is that English pubs facilitate a distinctive form of egalitarianism that runs counter to everyday life because the normal rules about politeness and restraint are suspended. Australian pubs don't require this suspension in the same way, given that 'polite' and 'restrained' aren't two words typically associated with Australian identity.†

†Australians tend to valorize the figure of the 'larrikin'—a boisterous, irreverent (read: badly behaved) bloke with a disregard for convention and authority. Larrikinism is rampant in Australians who travel overseas, who often feel like they have a reputation to live up to—or down to, as it were. 'JAFA' and 'NAFA' ('Just Another Fucking Aussie' and 'Not Another Fucking Aussie') are terms coined by Brits overexposed to Australian larrikins, although the expressions have more recently been exported to Canada, in tandem with the arrival of hordes of young Australians on work-travel visas.

**Actually, even people who don't set themselves above others are often cut down regardless, the mere existence of these attributes often being enough to convey the impression that the holder looks down upon others. This results in a widespread cultural tendency to criticize anyone who is successful, regardless of how modest they are—a phenomenon known as 'Tall poppy syndrome'. The primary exception is sporting figures, who are generally immune from such criticisms because they are seen to come by their success through natural, 'God-given' talent (the training and drive required to become an elite athlete being considered a minor detail). The cricketer Sir Donald Bradman has basically reached the Australian equivalent of sainthood, and has the coins and stamps bearing his image to prove it.

departs from English ideals of politeness, restraint, and class-consciousness. For example, when our former Prime Minister Paul Keating made a speech highlighting his republican tendencies during the Queen's state visit to Australia in 1992, and then compounded the insult by putting his arm around her, the English tabloids had a collective conniption fit.

These cultural ideals are reflected in miniature in the shout, which places drinkers into equivalent relation, thereby reinforcing a shared collective identity as equals. This is because all people are equal in the shout, and all shouts are equal, regardless of the amount of money any individual expends during their round. However, it's worth noting that the ideology of the shout often departs from its reality. As the linguist Anna Wierzbicka notes, there is often a competitive dimension to the shout. Moreover, many Australians feel ambivalent about the practice—a 2017 national survey found that most people (81%) disliked the obligation to participate in the shout. The reasons they gave for this were multiple: respondents complained that they knew people who didn't return shouts, they often spent more than they could afford, and mostly ended up drinking more than they wanted. Indeed, the ideology of the shout disguises the fact that participants are acutely aware of matters of cost. Because the shout is a form of balanced reciprocity, resentments quickly build if a participant consistently orders more expensive drinks (wine, cocktails, etc.) rather than a beer, the traditional drink of choice.*

The sense of constraint and obligation embedded in the shout is precisely what explains the relative absence of

---

*Based on Kate Fox's observations, similar rules apply in round buying in the UK, and that is certainly my experience.

reciprocal round buying in the USA.* According to James Carrier, the perfect gift for Americans is supposed to be an unfettered expression of personal affection, with no regard for price on either the part of the giver or the recipient, and no expectation of a return gift (aside from a simple 'thank you'). In Carrier's words, 'The gift is free, the recipient is without obligation, the thing given is wholly the recipient's'. Although the American ideal of the free gift is clearly a fiction,** Carrier suggests that it was a way of reconciling the nature of gift exchange with American cultural understandings of the individual. Just as Americans are considered to be free, independent, and autonomous agents, the gifts they give are likewise seen to be free and independent of obligation. If gifts *required* reciprocation, this would compromise the recipient's autonomy because they would be indebted to the giver until the gift was returned—an idea repugnant to American sensibilities.

Anna Wierzbicka has observed that while Australians prize mateship and the associated values of loyalty, solidarity, and mutual support, Americans value self-reliance as a cultural ideal. Thus, the American Dream 'of rising from the log cabin to the White House' is not one shared by many Australians, who see the individual as only rising within the collective. Indeed, the differences based on wealth and education that Australians are taught to down-

---

*Indeed, US bars are poorly equipped to deal with reciprocally purchased rounds, because they generally provide table service. The allure of my 'exotic' Australian accent wore off very quickly when the waitress had to figure out who owed what for the bill, given that my round of beers disrupted the individual tabs she was keeping for customers. Her goodwill had dispelled entirely by my second visit, probably in part because of the measly size of my prior tip.

**Interestingly, it's a fiction that is built into MS Word's grammar check function, which treats 'free gift' as redundant and patronizingly suggests that 'more concise language would be clearer for your reader'.

play are actively cultivated in the USA:* 'tall poppies' are celebrated rather than denigrated because they are living proof that the American Dream can be realized. This is why buying a round for the entire bar is acceptable. As a symbol of individual celebration and success it helps maintain the ideology of the perfect gift, because the one-off nature of the gesture allows the pretence of the unfettered gift to be maintained. However, when someone wants to pick up the tab again and again, the pretence is harder to maintain, and the recipient starts feeling annoyed and resentful. Reciprocal round buying is even worse—by obligating a response in kind, it shatters the illusion entirely.

In sum, while we live in a system based on commodity exchange, a good portion of our lives involve gift exchanges—interactions where objects are embedded in social relationships and impact them in all sorts of subtle ways. As I learned the hard way, even in the innocuous setting of a local tavern, gift-giving is a fraught experience if you don't know the underlying cultural rules at play. Moreover, rules around drinking provide a valuable lens into cultural conceptions of the individual and the collective—and the desired relationship between them. To quote Mary Douglas, 'profound insights into the nature of solidarity and trust can be expected from applying the theory of the gift to ourselves'. Undoubtedly my colleagues were as relieved as I was when I stopped turning up to the FAC. Still, little did they know that if they'd just bought me a damn drink, a long and fruitful relationship could have been established.

---

*The Irish singer Bono captured the distinctiveness of this American vision of success in his observation that, 'In the United States, you look at the guy that lives in the mansion on the hill, and you think, you know, "one day, if I work really hard, I could live in that mansion." In Ireland, people look up at the guy in the mansion on the hill and go, "one day, I'm going to get that bastard".'

11

You Can't Say 'C*nt' in Canada

My husband and I are both prolific swearers—a trait shared by many of our fellow Australians.* However, there is one word that I am somewhat less inclined to use than my husband. When I was growing up, 'cunt' was strongly gendered in its usage. Boys in my high school frequently employed it, but its usage was far less common amongst girls. In fact, when I was sixteen, all the girls in my grade were grilled by a teacher over the identity of a student who had graffitied the wall of a toilet stall with 'For all your bloody cunts'. She'd scrawled the words just above the disposal unit for tampons and sanitary pads, with an arrow helpfully pointing down, just in case there was some uncertainty about what she was referring to.

*The profligate nature of Australian swearing has been noted by various scholars. In *The Anatomy of Swearing*, the anthropologist Ashley Montagu observed that, 'The white Australian... numbers among his fellows perhaps the most inveterate and unimaginative swearers that exist anywhere in the world today'. The philologist Sidney Baker likewise noted that, 'Australians do not use more vulgarisms than the English and Americans. They merely use some of those vulgarisms more often'. (I'm not entirely convinced that the former is true, but the latter definitely is.)

We all knew who the culprit was but pretended igno-rance. Beyond the fact that no one wanted to be a snitch, the offence didn't seem that bad; I mean, in one sense, it could be read as a literal description of the purpose of the unit, which typically doesn't carry any identifying marks. Angered by our recalcitrance, the teacher insisted that 'cunt' was a deeply offensive term and that the culprit had demeaned herself and the rest of us by using it. Given that variants of 'Johnny is a cunt' were presumably scrawled all over the boys' toilet stalls, the teacher's concern seemed to stem from the fact that the term had been used in a liter-al rather than metaphoric sense and that the offence had been committed in the girls' toilets, rather than the boys'.

This struck me as rather sexist* and, if anything, made me more inclined to want to use the term myself—although this didn't happen until I entered university, and my initial attempts were extremely awkward, given that I lacked the sangfroid to employ it casually. However, that changed after I met my husband,** for whom 'cunt' is

*However, it's worth noting that women tend to use weaker expletives than men—a difference first highlighted by the linguist Robin Lakoff in her 1975 book *Language and Women's Place*. Interestingly, the pattern has continued to broadly hold despite the widespread normalization of swearing and changing valuations of its offensiveness. Michael Gauth-ier and Adrien Guille studied language use on Twitter amongst users in England between the ages of twelve and thirty, focusing on the tweet frequency of twenty-six common swear words. They found that the two words most commonly used by boys and men across age groups were 'fuck' and 'cunt' and the term most used by girls and women was 'bitch'. Interestingly, gender norms around swearing have also been reported historically and cross-culturally, although the topic is not well studied enough to determine whether this pattern is universal.

**My husband insists that an early conversation we had about the term convinced him of my viability as a prospective partner. That said, since the publication of Germaine Greer's *The Female Eunuch*, reclaiming the term has become a common rite amongst budding feminists. In a typi-

an all-purpose swear word: a term of deep affection and intense annoyance, a noun but also an adjective (cunty, cuntish, cuntful), and an expression that can refer to both people and objects alike (for example, cars can be cunts; so too can washing machines or indeed any object that isn't behaving in the manner you would like). Over time, I became so inured to the term that I started thoughtlessly using it myself, albeit mostly in its adjectival form and primarily in contexts reserved for what I considered to be truly obnoxious behaviour (as in 'that's a really cunty thing to do'). And then we moved to Canada.

The Australian comedian Kevin Bloody Wilson has a song titled *You Can't Say Cunt in Canada*, which he wrote after being informed by an official from the Canadian consulate that he would only obtain a travel visa to do his R-rated comedy show in Canada if he refrained from using the term; naturally, he opened his first show in Toronto with the song. But the song isn't remotely hyperbolic: you really *can't* say cunt in Canada.* Although the linguists Keith Allan and Kate Burridge assert in *Forbidden Words: Taboo and the Censoring of Language* that it is generally accepted that 'cunt' is the most taboo word in English, this

---

cal example of the genre, Erin McKelle highlights the misogyny in the taboo surrounding the term, stating, 'All it means is "vagina". Get over it'. These kinds of pieces are common enough that they have sparked various satires—such as a piece published in *Reductress* titled, 'How I reclaimed the word "cunt" by being one'. The article begins, 'For too long, the word "cunt" has been a total taboo, often thought to be too harsh or horrible to describe women with, but not anymore. I took it in my own hands to reclaim the word cunt by being the cuntiest cunt there ever was, and I'm proud to say it worked. You're welcome, world'.

*When I unthinkingly referred to someone's behaviour as 'cunty' in a conversation with a friend and colleague, shocked silence followed; I learned after that to avoid the term in public. My husband, it must be said, took much longer.

is arguably more true of American and Canadian English than the Australian and British variants. Indeed, in *Rooted: An Australian History of Bad Language*, the historian and lexicographer Amanda Laugesen observes that the term has effectively become a culturally normalized 'Australianism' in recent years. To quote the linguist Nick Nicholas, 'it is mostly a more vulgar counterpart of the Australian term bastard, and it almost always refers to men rather than women. Just like bastard, if it is qualified by an adjective, it is typically informal, jocular, or dismissive, rather than outright offensive, in "lower" social contexts'. *BuzzFeed* and the *Outback Dictionary* both highlight the potentially positive connotations of the term, especially as a synonym for 'mate'. However, as Nicholas notes, its jocular form is reserved primarily for men.*

As numerous linguists and scholars have shown, 'cunt' wasn't originally an offensive term in English. According to Allan and Burridge, it was a well-established word in Early Middle English and turned up in everything from place names (e.g., Gropecuntlane—a common name for disreputable lovers' lanes or red-light districts) to surnames, including Godwin Glawecuncte, Simon Sitbithecunte, and Bele Wydecunthe.** It also appeared in Lanfranc's

---

*Unlike my husband's communications with his own brothers, I don't begin every message to my brother with the greeting 'Oi, cunt!' I suppose that women could theoretically call men cunts in a jocular fashion, but this usage seems to be primarily by men, for men. However, this isn't necessarily due to the genital-based and gendered nature of the insult, which is strongly downplayed in Australian usage—the jocular form of 'bastard' follows similar rules (i.e., female friends don't generally greet each other with that term either).

**Bele Wydecunthe would be a marvellous name for an *Austin Powers* or *James Bond* character but would automatically incur an R rating in the USA, unlike Alotta Fagina or Pussy Galore. The Motion Picture Association of America's famously obtuse rating system states that PG-13 films

Science of Cirgurie, which includes the following statement, 'In wymmen the necke of the bladdre is schort, & is maad fast to the cunte'. However, Kate Burridge notes that by the 1700s, it had clearly fallen out of favour. While the term appeared in the *Universal Etymological English Dictionary,* published in 1721, its definition was camouflaged in Latin as *Pudendum Muliebre.* Likewise, it was included in the 4,000 terms in the *Dictionary of the Vulgar Tongue,* published in 1785, but the entry was written as follows: 'c**t: a nasty word for a nasty thing'.

Various plant names got a makeover as well—according to the sociologist Piers Beirne, 'cuntehoare' (along with 'priests' ballocks' and 'prick madam') was stricken from the botanical record during this period. It soon became so linguistically taboo that it caused collateral damage—Burridge notes that 'coney' (pronounced like 'honey' and sometimes written as 'cunny'), a widespread term for rabbit, fell out of favour in the nineteenth century because of its awkward linguistic associations with 'cunt'.* In consequence, 'cunt'

---

only allow 'single use of one of the harsher sexually derived words, though only as an expletive... More than one such expletive requires an R rating, as must even one of those words used in a sexual context'. To translate: one 'fuck' is okay, as long as it doesn't refer to actual fucking. However, the same rule doesn't seem to apply to 'cunt'. Indeed, the Edgar Wright films *Hot Fuzz* and *The World's End,* which include several humorous uses of the term, were both given an R rating in the USA. Notably, they were not similarly penalized in the UK, where they were legally viewable by over fifteens, based on the recognition that the contexts of usage were not 'aggressive or threatening or complicated by any kind of power imbalance'.

*The same trend is evident for words like 'cock', 'ass', 'bitch' and 'pussy'—not coincidentally, all are terms that involve what the anthropologist Edmund Leach referred to as animal abuse. As these terms moved from the animal to the human realm, they became less common to describe the former, although the degree to which this replacement has occurred differs from country to country. Thus, 'cock' in Australia

was banished from the English language until the 1960s, when the Crown Prosecution in the UK unsuccessfully brought charges against Penguin under the Obscene Publications Act for publishing *Lady Chatterley's Lover*.

Although no one has come up with a satisfactory explanation for why the status of the term changed so radically, Piers Beirne suggests that it was likely connected with the broader cultural shifts Norbert Elias described in *The Civilizing Process*. In effect, the expanding threshold of repugnance around natural bodily functions extended to the words for describing them, requiring them to be veiled in euphemism. In support of this theory, 'fuck' was another casualty of the period—according to Geoffrey Hughes, it was unlisted in standard dictionaries from 1728 until 1965. However, like 'cunt', it is found in several English names from the thirteenth century, such as Ric Wyndfuk, although there is little evidence of the use of the term to describe sexual intercourse (or at least bawdy activities) before the fifteenth century.*

The waxing and waning status of obscenities illustrates a key challenge with studying swearing: like pornography, we know it when we see it, but it is extremely difficult to objectively define.** Typically, swear words are character-

---

refers to penises rather than roosters, and 'pussy' in the USA refers to vaginas rather than cats—as I learned when I was ten, living in the USA with my family, and drew a picture of a 'pretty little pussy' for my classmates.

*For the record, in *The F-Word*, the lexicographer Jesse Sheidlower roundly dismisses the popular theory that fuck began life as an acronym: 'For Unlawful Carnal Knowledge' (or, in some accounts, 'Forced Unsolicited Carnal Knowledge'). Instead, he suggests that its origins are Germanic and relate to several words that literally mean 'to strike' or to 'move back and forth', but simultaneously have sexual connotations.

**The 'I know it when I see it' expression comes from Justice Potter

ized as those words that are offensive, stigmatized, taboo, and inappropriate, and that convey strong emotion. However, as the linguists Kristy Beers Fägersten and Karyn Stapleton note, the subjective dimension of these concepts results in a definition vulnerable to over-inclusion. For example, while 'bloody' and 'bugger' are generally considered swear words, most Australians don't treat them as such. The terms have been widely used in television ads since the 1990s,* and their usage is uniformly distributed across the population—from old ladies to youngish children.** According to the linguist Anna Wierzbicka, they form part of a quartet of 'b' words (along with 'bastard' and 'bullshit') central to Australian English. In her words, 'Elsewhere, they are regarded as "coarse slang", but in Australia, they are part of everyday language'.

Complicating matters further, in languages with hon-

Stewart's 1964 Supreme Court ruling on Jacobellis v. Ohio, where obscenity charges had been brought against the manager of a movie theatre for showing Louise Malle's film *The Lovers*. In discussing how hard-core pornography should be defined, Justice Stewart noted, 'I shall not today attempt to further define the kinds of material I understand to be embraced within that shorthand description, and perhaps I could never succeed in intelligibly doing so. But I know it when I see it'.

*The catchphrase of drink driving ads in the 1990s was 'If you drink then drive, you're a bloody idiot'. There was also a very popular Toyota Hilux ad in the late 1990s featuring farmers declaring 'bugger!' and 'bugger me!' after underestimating the power of their utility vehicle in various amusing mishaps. Interestingly, the ad was from New Zealand, where it attracted hundreds of complaints; it aired without any issues in Australia.

**This wasn't always the case in Australia. My father, whose formative years were in the 1950s, tells a story from his childhood about getting angry with his father over some perceived offence, and then marching out on the street to yell out every swear word he knew—'shit', 'poo', 'bloody', 'bugger', and 'bastard' being about the extent of what his five-year-old vocabulary could conjure. He was soundly belted for his trouble.

orifics and formal and informal terms of address, it is the tone* and degree of formality used that often determine whether language is offensive. For example, the linguist Senko Maynard notes that in Japan, blunt sentence endings can be just as rude as actual swear words, making terms that seem relatively innocuous in English deeply insulting—like 'you idiot' (*bakkayaroo*). This is also true of Korean; telling someone to 'go away' or 'get lost' in its blunt form (*kkeojyeo*) is almost as offensive as 'fuck off' in English. Context is also critical to understanding the varied meanings of the term 'pardon' in England. According to the anthropologist Kate Fox, it is a far greater linguistic offence amongst the upper and upper-middle classes than uttering actual obscenities. Apparently, the author Jilly Cooper once overheard her son telling a friend, 'Mummy says that "pardon" is a much worse word than "fuck".' The contextual nuances of swearing, therefore, mean that it's difficult to generalize about its nature or frequency beyond the fact that it appears to be a universal human trait.**

So why do we swear? In *The Anatomy of Swearing*, the anthropologist Ashley Montagu argued that 'It is as old as man and coeval with language'. He suggested that swear-

---

*The problem is greatly exacerbated with tonal languages. The anthropologist Nigel Barley, in discussing his fieldwork amongst the Dowayo in Cameroon, highlights his difficulties with grappling with the language, noting, 'My rather wobbly control of the language was also a grave danger. Obscenity is never very far away in Dowayo. A shift of tone changes the interrogative particle, attached to a sentence to convert it into a question, into the lewdest word in the language, something like "cunt". I would, therefore, baffle and amuse Dowayos by greeting them, "Is the sky clear for you, cunt?"'

**Based on a claim made by Montagu, it's frequently asserted that Native Americans, Japanese, Malayans, and Polynesians don't have native swear words. This is demonstrably false, but in Montagu's defence, almost nothing had been written about swearing at the time, the subject matter not being deemed appropriate for scholarly study.

ing, with its capacity to express strong emotion, is a valuable mechanism for letting off steam, acting as a social safety valve for societies. These ideas have been explored at length in *Swearing is Good for You: The Amazing Science of Bad Language* by the neuropsychologist Emma Byrne, who suggests that swearing acts as a physical safety valve as well as a social one. As she discusses, there is experimental evidence that swearing increases our ability to tolerate pain. For example, British undergraduate students asked to stick their hands in ice-cold water could do it for 50% longer if they said things like 'Arrgh, no, fuck, bugger, shit' (or variants thereof) throughout the process. However, the *type* of swearing was important; minced oaths (i.e., euphemisms) like 'fudge', 'blighter', and 'shoot' didn't work as well. 'Stronger swearwords are stronger painkillers', Byrne concludes. She suggests this is because swearing has physiological effects on the body, increasing heart rate and impacting emotions such as fear and aggression that moderate pain.

These effects highlight the involvement of the brain in swearing. Language is associated with the left hemisphere of the brain, so it shouldn't be a surprise that brain injuries to this area impact speech. But what's particularly interesting is the type of speech they affect. In particular, people with injuries to this side of the brain often struggle with regular words but become more prone to spouting involuntary obscenities. The neuropsychologist Shlomit Finkelstein suggests this is because the left hemisphere is implicated in intentional propositional speech, whereas the right hemisphere is implicated in automatic speech, including swearing. According to Byrne, one of the earliest documented cases is that of Phineas Gage, a nineteenth-century American railway foreman involved in an industrial accident that saw him end up with a metal rod through his left frontal lobe. Although he miraculously survived the accident, he suffered various effects from his injury, including a new propensity to indulge in what his doctors called 'the grossest profanity'.

Similar patterns have been noted as a result of aphasia, which is generally caused by damage to the left hemisphere. For example, one patient both Finkelstein and Byrne discuss, who had had the entire left side of his brain removed, could swear far more easily than he could manage other types of words. Moreover, the slurring of his voice was less apparent when he swore, and swearing seemed to help him speak more fluently. Such cases would suggest that swearing may be significant to language and human evolution in ways we don't fully understand. To quote Byrne, 'I don't think we would have made it as the world's most populous primate if we hadn't learned to swear... swearing helps us deal better with our pain and frustration, it helps to build tighter social groups, and it's a good sign that we might be about to snap, which means that it forestalls violence'.

Further support for the connection between swearing and human evolution is that nonhuman primates seem to have the same rudimentary capacities for swearing that they do for language—at least, based on attempts to teach chimpanzees American Sign Language. The findings of these studies are controversial, with many animal researchers claiming that chimps' capacity to learn signs results more from conditioning than language acquisition per se. However, one of the most successful experiments was with Washoe, a female chimpanzee trained by Allen and Beatrice Gardner in the late 1960s. Washoe had learned 130 signs by the age of five and soon started to combine them in unexpected ways, demanding that her trainers 'gimme sweet' and 'come open'. When she saw other juvenile chimps upset, Washoe would often sign 'come hug'; on one occasion, she signed 'cry me me hurt' in response to a favoured human absenting herself from a training session. After she was toilet trained, Washoe spontaneously started to use 'dirty' as an insult, saying things like 'dirty Jack gimme drink' when a trainer refused to obey her request and 'dirty monkey' when scared by an aggressive macaque.

Washoe's actions are significant because 'dirty' words referring to the genitals, sexual intercourse, and excretion seem common to swearing across many cultures and languages. In light of Mary Douglas's argument that the margins of the body and its effluvia are frequently tabooed because they are seen as powerful and polluting, it makes sense that words associated with the body's margins are themselves symbolically charged.* This is especially true when such words are used figuratively rather than literally. Indeed, numerous linguists suggest that part of what defines a swear word is using the term in a non-literal way. Telling someone to 'go fuck yourself', for example, is not an injunction to masturbate.** This explains why certain terms describing the body's margins (and the acts and emissions emanating from it) are more stigmatized

---

*Of course, these aren't the only tabooed words. Another pattern that has been identified is the use of swear words relating to the sacred, i.e., blasphemy. However, these words are obviously much more culturally specific in form. As societies become more secular, such terms tend to lose their force. In the Middle Ages, it was a far greater offence to take the Lord's name in vain than to use 'dirty' words; the opposite is generally true in Anglophone countries today.

**As Bill Bryson has observed, 'It is a strange and little-noted idiosyncrasy of our tongue that when we wish to express extreme fury we entreat the object of our rage to undertake an anatomical impossibility, or, stranger still, to engage in the one activity that is bound to give him more pleasure than anything else. Can there be, when you think about it, a more improbable sentiment than "Get fucked!" We might as well snarl, "Make a lot of money!" or "Have a nice day!"'

than others.

Here, it's helpful to consider Allan and Burridge's distinction between orthophemisms, euphemisms, and dysphemisms, which, simply put, can be characterized respectively as straight-talking, sweet-talking, and talking offensively. For example, 'faeces' is an orthophemism, 'poo' is a euphemism, and 'shit' is a dysphemism. Although they refer to the same object, 'faeces' isn't a swear word, but 'shit' is, and we call people we want to insult 'shitheads' rather than 'faeces-heads'.* This is arguably because we have evolved a particular vocabulary for bodily parts, acts, and emanations when we want to employ them as insults,** which is why it's far less meaningful to call someone a 'vagina' than a 'cunt', or a 'penis' than a 'dick', or a 'buttocks' than an 'arse'***—you can do it, but it doesn't seem offensive so much as odd. Relatedly, I imagine that telling someone 'sex you' or 'go have sex with yourself' would produce stares of blank incomprehension.

In sum, although swearing has a bad reputation, it's mostly undeserved. Instead, it's best considered a fascinat-

---

*'Poo-head' is possible, and more recognizably insulting than 'faeces-head', but sounds like the sort of thing a five-year-old would say.

**This is why people often find it particularly shocking when dysphemisms are used descriptively—such as using the word 'cunt' to describe a vagina (as my classmate did), or 'fuck' to describe sex. The use of these terms is expected to be restricted to non-literal contexts, and it's therefore jarring when they are used as orthophemisms instead. At least, that is the only explanation I can come up with for the Motion Picture Association of America's distinction between sexually-derived words used as expletives vs using them in a sexual context, and their stricter ratings for the latter.

***These terms illustrate a common trait of dysphemisms: they are more likely to be one-syllable words than their orthophemistic counterparts, which is why 'four-letter words' is a common euphemism for swear words.

ing and complex part of human language—one that was probably built in from the outset. In swearing, we simultaneously see our basest instincts at play, but also the human capacity for creativity—as numerous commentators have observed, there are few words in the English language more versatile than 'fuck'.* But swearing is also slippery. Given that one man's 'fudge' is another man's 'fuck', it's never entirely clear what words will offend: when it comes to swearing, tone, timing, and context are everything (unless, obviously, you say 'cunt' in Canada). According to Fägersten and Stapleton, it's precisely this variability that keeps things interesting—if its usage and reception were predictable, swearing would involve no risks but none of its many benefits. In fact, swearing probably falls into the category of indispensable acts and objects that we would have had to invent if they didn't already exist. As Emma Byrne notes, 'We need swearing and, however we might have invented it, I'm fucking glad that we did'.

---

*Indeed, the transgressive power of the word seems to now be carrying over to other languages—it is one of the few swear words that has effectively globalized. 'Cunt' has not travelled so well.

12

Cack Hands and Southpaws

When I was doing fieldwork in South Korea in the
late 1990s, foreigners weren't a particularly common
sight in the country, and my appearance invariably drew
attention. But the single physical attribute that was most
commented upon was my left-handedness. Whenever anyone saw me writing in my fieldnote book, they would invariably exclaim that I was *oensonjabi*: a left-hander.* Yet,
despite the novelty of seeing a left-handed writer in action, no one was surprised by it, the assumption being
that Westerners are commonly left-handed. My attempts
to explain that only about 10% of people are left-handed
the world over, so countries like Australia and the USA
were hardly teeming with lefties, fell on largely deaf ears.
It seemed that for most people, my foreignness and my
left-handedness went together.

The only overtly left-handed Korean I met was the
British-educated daughter of a Korean and British couple.

*This appears to be a common experience for left-handers prone to
writing in notebooks in public spaces in foreign lands. In his book *A
Left-Hand Turn Around the World*, the journalist (and lefty) David Wolman
recounts similar reactions while on assignment in Moscow.

The girl's parents had made the conscious choice to allow her to use her preferred hand rather than correcting the 'defect', as was standard at the time. Even today, the rate of left-handed writers in South Korea remains extremely low—according to a 2017 article in *The Korea Times*, about 1% of Koreans use their left hand to write, and only 4% use their left hand to eat with chopsticks. Indeed, being left-handed in Korea poses daily challenges—primarily because it's considered rude to give or accept items with your left hand. The right hand should be used, or the right hand with the left hand supporting it if you want to be super-polite. I was constantly afraid of causing offence because of my instinctive tendency to use my left hand, whether handing a shopkeeper money or accepting a gift from a friend.

While living in South Korea made me acutely self-conscious about my left-handedness, it was also part of my background experience growing up. This is because kids learn pretty young that right-handedness is normal and left-handedness is not. For example, friends in London had assumed that their five-year-old son was left-handed because this is the hand he uses for most activities at home; however, they recently learned that he has been using his right hand at school. When they quizzed him about this, he told them that this was his 'school' hand—presumably based on the observation that this is the hand most students in his class use.

I was never so self-aware or observant as a five-year-old, but I recall that it wasn't much fun being a left-hander when I started school in Australia in the early 1980s. Unlike my parents' generation, I wasn't forced to use my right hand, but teachers constantly corrected how I held my pencil to mimic the stance of right-handers. Although a basic lesson in human anatomy should make it abundantly clear that left-handers can't hold their pencil the same way as right-handers because their hand has a completely different orientation to the page, for my teachers, the idea that the left hand should be the mirror image of the right was simply too strong to relinquish.

Writing was a distinct problem for me as a young child—not because I couldn't do it, but because I could only do it *backwards.* My earliest efforts, immortalized in relatives' guestbooks, were perfectly legible in a mirror but gibberish if read the usual way.* I got the hang of writing in the 'right' direction once I started school, but my teachers' criticisms of my technique never extended to showing me anything useful—such as how to avoid smudging every sentence I wrote.** Beyond writing, I don't recall any other issues resulting from my left-handedness, although it was a handy excuse for my poor performance at various sports—whether it be ten-pin bowling, golf, or, I adamantly insisted, table tennis.*** However, I always notice other

*Sadly, this isn't a sign of incipient genius, as history's most famous mirror writer, Leonardo da Vinci, was a lefty as well as a savant. An overview by the neuropsychologist Geoffrey Schott suggests that left-handers have a natural facility for mirror writing, which is more of a motor skill than a cognitive one. This fits with my own experience—I can still mirror write fast and accurately as long as I don't think about it.

**Not a single left-hander I know holds their hand the same way. We all develop our own techniques for writing, from the wrist-twisters to the paper-turners to those who have the finger technique of a professional flautist. My own fist-like hold was the bane of my primary school teachers, although they never managed to cure me of the technique.

***For the record, being left-handed is often considered to be an advantage in interactive sports, because right-handers are less equipped to deal with the technique of left-handed opponents. The most extreme example of this advantage can be found in fencing, where between 35-45% of world champions are left-handed. Sadly, having very little hand-eye coordination, I have not personally found this to be the case. The one

left-handers and feel the irrepressible urge to inform them that I am a lefty* when in their presence. Apparently, this isn't uncommon—David Wolman labels this phenomenon 'the fraternity of the Southpaw' in his book *A Left-Hand Turn Around the World*.

While I've always found the topic of handedness personally fascinating, it's also extremely significant anthropologically. Although the source of some debate within the discipline, handedness appears to be largely distinct to humans and the human line. A review of the evidence published in the *Journal of Anthropological Sciences* suggests that right-handed preference was firmly established by the appearance of Neanderthals, based on evidence from tool use and cave art. However, we don't fully understand why that is—although various theories exist.

---

time I have ever come close to winning a table tennis match against my husband occurred when he played left-handed (unbeknownst to me)—something my father pointed out when he came to watch our match. Even more galling than the fact that my husband had chosen to give himself a handicap was that I didn't win the match.

*This is a trait that political lefties seem to share with physical ones. In case you're wondering about how and why the terms 'left' and 'right' came to be widely used political designations, in *Wrong Turnings: How the Left Got Lost*, Geoffrey Hodgson writes that the metaphor was introduced in the French National Assembly of 1789: those deputies critical of the monarchy congregated to the seats on the left of the President's chair and those who supported the aristocracy and monarchy were seated on the right side. However, this seems to be more of a post-hoc justification—after all, from the perspective of the President himself, the dissenters would have been on his right side and the supporters on his left. Instead, it made cultural sense for the non-dominant position to be called the 'left' and the dominant position to be called the 'right' because of the pre-existing meanings of these concepts. In this context, the meaning of the terms, like the use of the terms 'bull' and 'bear' to describe the stock market, stems primarily from their utility as a way of conceptualizing and talking about difference—their meaning is relational rather than intrinsic.

According to some accounts, the predominance of right-handedness in humans and our direct ancestors must be due to some sort of evolutionary advantage it conferred, and various explanations have been posited to explain its adaptive value. For example, one early theory was that it evolved from warriors carrying their shields in their non-dominant hand; for right-handers, this meant their heart was more protected, thus increasing the chances of surviving battle. Another theory points to the tendency of human mothers to hold infants on the left side of their body based on the way in which the mother's heartbeat soothes the baby, which in turn leads to favouring the right hand. However, as the neuropsychologist Marietta Papadatou-Pastou states, in what amounts to a masterful understatement, 'These two theories, interesting as they might be, do not seem plausible'.

The most convincing explanation is that handedness is a by-product of the broader lateralization of the human brain that occurred as a result of language evolution and the cognitive asymmetries it engendered—especially the localization of language and speech functions in the left hemisphere.* This is why the evolutionary biologist Tecumseh Fitch and the primatologist Stephanie Braccini suggest that handedness is most likely a 'red herring'—an artefact of other processes rather than significant in its own right. Perhaps the most influential theory in explaining this is the psychologist Marian Annett's 'right shift' theory, which suggests that the dominant allele responsible for speech development in the left hemisphere leads to a higher probability of being right-handed. This inter-

---

*For the record, the language centre for left-handers typically resides in the left hemisphere. Our brains are not the mirror image of right-handers, as is sometimes assumed. As Wolman notes, 'most lefty brains are like righty brains, at least as far as speech function is concerned'.

relation between language and handedness is supported by the fact that our closest living primate relatives don't exhibit handedness to anywhere near the same degree as humans—although there is some evidence of nascent hand preference and task specialization in various species in much the same way that we see nascent evidence of language acquisition and swearing.

However, while the 'right shift' theory suggests a clear genetic component to handedness, empirical support is qualified. For example, we know that males are slightly more likely to be left-handed than females, although we don't understand why. Handedness also seems to run in families, with the children of left-handed parents somewhat more likely to be left-handed. Still, estimates differ dramatically on how much influence genetic inheritance has. According to the neuropsychologist Dorothy Bishop, one of the primary methodological issues is that family 'sinistrality'* is more likely to be found in people from large families. Thus, while two left-handers seem likelier to produce a left-handed child, this remains an extremely weak predictor of handedness.

The genetic basis of handedness gets even muddier when twins enter the picture. A recent analysis by Lena Pfeifer and her colleagues of the results of fifty-nine studies found that left-handedness seems more common in twins—including fraternal twins as well as identical ones, even though the former are no more genetically related than two regular siblings. While concordance rates are slightly higher in identical twins, the fact that identical twins are frequently *discordant* in their handedness clearly

---

*'Sinistral' is the technical name for a left-hander and 'dextral' for a right-hander. I will have more to say on their origins below, but, no, you're not imagining the negative and positive associations of the terms.

rules out any clear-cut genetic foundation for handedness. Moreover, Pfeifer and her colleagues found that differences in the rates of left-handedness between twins and singletons appear to be disappearing, given that many newer studies don't find a correlation.

A major problem with research in this area is how to define handedness. As it turns out, handedness is far more complicated to assess than we might assume. If asked, the average person would probably define handedness based on the hand they use to write with. But as I've already observed, this is a poor measure of natural handedness because cultural biases regarding handedness are frequently inflicted on writing practices. Also, how do you measure handedness if someone is from a non-literate culture? Task specialization? How many tasks would someone need to use the same hand for to constitute evidence of handedness? And should we be testing spontaneous handedness or the preferred hand for familiar activities?

These methodological issues partly explain why measures of handedness vary dramatically from study to study (and era to era). For example, according to Marchant and McGrew, anthropologists have reported rates of left-handedness ranging from 0.5% in Zaire to 22.8% amongst the Kwakiutl—a First Nations community from British Columbia.

The 1971 Edinburgh Handedness Inventory was the earliest attempt to try and resolve these issues. Developed by the experimental psychologist Carolus Oldfield, it involved assessing participants' overall handedness based on which hand they used (or which hand was dominant) for twenty discrete activities: writing, drawing, throwing, using scissors, a comb, a toothbrush, a knife without a fork, a spoon, a hammer, a screwdriver, a tennis racket, a knife with a fork, a cricket bat, a golf club, a broom, a rake, striking a match, opening a box, dealing cards, and threading a needle.

Somewhat unusually for an experimental scientist, Oldfield readily acknowledged the imperfect nature of the inventory. He openly wondered whether all items should be assigned the same ranking and was clearly aware of the culturally biased and gendered nature of various activities in the inventory. In his words,

> The British, for instance, have the odd habit of using their knife and fork at meal times simultaneously, and strongly enforced etiquette enjoins the holding of knife in the right, and the fork in the left, hand.* Cricket bats are not commonly used in Parisian suburbs, and many inhabitants of Manhattan apartment blocks find little use for rakes. While most men make shift to sew on indispensable buttons, the use of needle and thread is unquestionably far more prevalent among the female sex.

His conclusions regarding the utility of the inventory were strikingly modest and tentative. According to Oldfield, the inventory was far from ideal, primarily useful in providing a common standard for comparison, but probably not a sufficient means of assessing handedness in contexts where it actually mattered.

The inventory provides some insight into just how culturally loaded handedness is. It's very difficult to think of

---

*It's true that the British method requires right-handed eaters to hold the fork in their non-dominant hand, but it's surely more efficient than the American method (labelled by the American doyenne of manners, Emily Post, as the 'zig-zag' method but more popularly known as the 'cut and switch'), which requires a constant switching of the fork from the left to the right hand. As a left-hander, I can say that it's far more pleasant to sit at a crowded dinner table with people using their cutlery in the British rather than American style, which resolves the otherwise omnipresent elbow-bumping problem.

activities that aren't either culturally specific or gendered in their distribution (or both), or where the implements aren't designed in such a way that you are disadvantaged by using them left-handed* (e.g., scissors, golf clubs). Even universal activities like wiping one's arse are subject to explicit cultural influences: in India, for example, the left hand is ideally used for sanitization after defecating, sentiments also endorsed in the *Kitab Al-Taharah* (*The Book of Purification*) by the Muslim scholar ibn al-Hajjaj.

These definitional issues aren't just academic but directly impact assessments of the prevalence of left-handedness.** For example, the evolutionary biologists Michel Raymond and Dominique Pontier analysed data from studies involving fourteen countries and over a million individuals, using throwing and hammering as a proxy for

---

*Various household implements are designed in such a way that they are basically impossible to use left-handed—a standard can opener, for example. The crank is designed to be turned clockwise with the right hand, and that is the only way they are functionally operable.

**To provide another example, consider masturbation. It is natural and presumably universal; however, it is often culturally proscribed, making it a poor potential indicator of handedness. Although a group of enterprising scholars have recently confirmed in the journal *Laterality* that 'masturbation is lateralized in a similar way to other manual motor behaviours in left-handed and right-handed men and women', they found that women masturbate less than men, regardless of their handedness, which brings us right back to the gender problem. Complicating matters further is the phenomenon of 'non-dominant-hand wanking', which, at least according to *Vice*, is a thing. While this might be connected with the thrill of using a less familiar hand to manipulate one's genitals, I suspect that it's also related to the proportion of right-handers who masturbate while viewing porn on their computer, and the need to use their dominant hand to scroll with the mouse (unlike left-handers, most of whom have learned to use a mouse right-handed, because that's how it's typically set up by default). Is non-dominant-hand wanking a portent that technology is transforming the significance of handedness? Only time will tell.

handedness. They found that when left-handed throwers or hammerers are included in the mix, the evidence of left-handedness becomes stronger—instead of the usual 10%, it was pushed up to between 15 and 20%. This would suggest that rates of left-handedness might be higher if measured differently or if the cultural biases against it were reduced.

The role that cultural biases have on expressions of handedness was first theorized by the French sociologist Robert Hertz. In 1909, he published an essay arguing that the preponderance of right-handedness couldn't be presumed to be merely the natural product of organic asymmetry because it was often obligatory and imposed by coercion. In an intriguing analogy, he noted, 'The feelings of a left-hander in a backward society are analogous to those of an uncircumcised man in countries where circumcision is law. The fact is that righthandedness is not simply accepted, submitted to, like a natural necessity: it is an ideal to which everybody must conform and which society forces us to respect by positive sanctions'.* As Hertz observed, one logical response to asymmetry would be to exercise and train the non-dominant hand, thereby correcting the weakness. Instead, in most cultures, precisely the opposite occurs: right-handers are incapable of doing anything left-handed, while left-handers, of necessity, are often forced to become proficient at using both.**

---

*Given the vehemence of his writing about the plight of left-handers, I'd hazard a guess that Hertz was a lefty, although this is not something we have any record of as Hertz died in World War I at the age of thirty-three.

**This isn't the same thing as being ambidextrous, which theoretically means one is equally proficient with both hands.† Very few people are therefore genuinely ambidextrous, although many people favour different hands for different tasks.

Adding insult to injury, Hertz argued that not only is the right hand typically favoured, but left-handedness is associated with negative qualities—an attitude he suggested was so commonplace as to be virtually universal. As Hertz observed, examples of the veneration of the right side over the left abound cross-culturally. This has been confirmed in subsequent anthropological scholarship, especially Rodney Needham's edited volume *Right and Left: Essays on Dual Symbolic Classification*, which introduced Hertz's work to English-speaking audiences. Contributors provide ample illustrations of the symbolic significance of the left-right dualism in East Africa, China, South-East Asia, and South India, with discussions of ancient Greek and Arabic traditions thrown in for good measure.

Judeo-Christian mythology is also rife with similar dualisms. Some of the symbolism is subtle—such as Jesus sitting at God's right hand and the tendency to depict Judas as a lefty*—but there's plenty of Old Testament bluntness as well: 'A wise man's heart inclines him to the right, but a fool's heart to the left' warns Ecclesiastes. This symbolism has carried over to the secular realm—after all, right hands are joined in marriage, take oaths, conclude contracts, and lend assistance. Conversely, the left side is associated with the deficient, profane, and impure—prejudices that are reflected in the very words we use to describe handedness. The technical terms for left and right-handedness, 'sinistral' and 'dextral', have the same Latin roots as 'sinister' and

---

†Actually, never sparing an opportunity to stick the knife in, ambidextrous literally means 'right-handed on both sides'.

*Judas is sometimes depicted as a lefty,† and a redhead to boot, presumably to ram home his villainy.

†The same types who think that *The Da Vinci Code* is a work of non-fiction speculate that Da Vinci depicted Judas as a left-hander in *The Last Supper*, clearly forgetting that Da Vinci was a lefty himself.

'dexterous', meaning unlucky/left and skilful/right. The term 'left' comes from Old English *luft*, meaning 'weak, foolish', and is related to the East Frisian *luf* and the Dutch dialectical *loof*, both of which similarly mean 'weak' and 'worthless'. The Goths termed the left side *lkudumei*, which meant 'weakest' and 'most crooked', and the Italian term is *manco*, which developed from 'crippled, deficient'. As David Wolman notes in *A Left-Hand Turn Around the World*, 'From an etymological perspective, the roots of the word left are just about as depressing as it gets'.

So why is the left hand so reviled? According to Hertz, this stems from the essential dualism of human thought—a view later elaborated on by the French anthropologist Claude Lévi-Strauss, whose work I've discussed at length. For Hertz, nature presents itself in the form of dualisms: night and day, light and dark, north and south, east and west, sky and earth, and so on. The law of polarity that governs the natural world is understood to govern the body as well—male vs female, right vs left, active vs passive, strong vs weak, and sacred vs profane. Thus, the right side is associated with the male, the active, the strong, and the sacred, and the left side is associated with the female, the passive, the weak, and the profane. In his words, 'it has its domain where it is mistress and from which the right hand is excluded; but this is a dark and ill-famed region. The power of the left hand is always somewhat occult and illegitimate; it inspires terror and repulsion'. This association of the left hand with the profane side of life, he argued, is why most societies paralyse the left hand while developing the right. Indeed, Hertz famously argued that our tendency towards dualism was so great that 'if organic asymmetry had not existed, it would have had to be invented'.

Of course, times have changed insofar as left-handedness has become significantly less stigmatized in the more than hundred-odd years since Hertz wrote his essay—even in those contexts, like South Korea, where it remains rare. But there's no question that lefties live in a world that wasn't physically designed for us—from the location of doorknobs to the design of the average office desk to the placement of the number pad on a keyboard. This is, I suspect, the source of all the unsupported rumours about the heightened creativity and intelligence of left-handers. As lefties living in a right-handed world, the simple truth is that most of us secretly (or not-so-secretly) feel superior to our right-handed brethren. Because we might not be any smarter, but we're certainly more *dexterous*, so we know that we're the 'right' handers after all.

13

The Magic of Numbers

When we moved to Vancouver and were looking for a place to live, we viewed listings in dozens of high-rise condos in the downtown area and quickly noticed a pattern: many were missing a designated fourth floor.* This was particularly evident in newer condos built after the turn of the twenty-first century. Confused about why this was, we asked our realtor and were informed that this was because the number four is considered unlucky by Chinese buyers. The words for 'four' and 'death' are homophones (i.e., they have the same pronunciation), which is

---

*The unlucky connotations of four are also found in North Asian countries like Japan and Korea, both of which incorporate Chinese scripts in their writing systems in the form of Kanji and Hanja, respectively. However, I must confess that I was unaware of this while living in Korea—probably because many buildings have a designated fourth floor (in fact, I lived in a fourth-floor apartment during my first year of fieldwork). I'm also not convinced that the superstition is as strong in Korea as in China. It's worth noting that Koreans use a Chinese-derived counting system in some contexts (e.g., money, years) and their native Korean system for others (e.g., age, objects) and the homophonic connection between 'four' and 'death' only occurs when the Sino-Korean term is used.

why it's common for buildings in Hong Kong, mainland China, and various other parts of North Asia to lack an explicit fourth and fourteenth floor.*

In response to the wave of immigration from Hong Kong after the handover to China in 1997, and the subsequent influx of migrants from mainland China, Vancouver condo developers had therefore accommodated the belief in much the same way they had dealt with longstanding superstitions about the number thirteen: by simply removing the offending numerals from signage and elevator panels. Some of the newer condos we looked at were missing a fourth, thirteenth, and fourteenth floor, causing buildings with twelve storeys to magically appear as if they had fifteen when you stepped in the elevator.

While one might be forgiven for thinking that such moves are merely wishful thinking on the part of real estate developers aiming to make their properties more attractive to buyers, this kind of number avoidance is common across a wide variety of contexts. Many major airlines skip the row thirteen, and most also avoid using it in their flight numbers based on the assumption that customers will be reluctant to travel on a flight so labelled. Likewise, Cathay Pacific, Hong Kong Airlines, and United Airlines skip the fourth row to accommodate North Asian preferences.

Moreover, superstitions about these numbers appear to have genuine effects on consumers' decisions—a phenomenon the psychologist Richard Wiseman discusses at length in *Quirkology: The Curious Science of Everyday Lives*. For example, in a national survey of American real estate agents, 40% said buyers were often triskaidekaphobic (i.e., resistant to buying a property numbered thirteen), causing sell-

---

*According to *Rogerson's Book of Numbers*, fourteen is even worse than four, sounding something like 'guaranteed death'.

ers to have to lower their property price. Likewise, a British study found that there were significantly lower traffic flows on sections of London's M25 motorway on Friday the 13th compared to Friday the 6th, which the researchers concluded was due to superstitious anxieties about travelling on the day.* A similar pattern holds for four. Studies of license plate auctions in Hong Kong and real estate transactions in Vancouver and Seattle found that plates and houses carrying the number four were significantly discounted in their sales price, although those containing an eight sold at a premium. The researchers attribute this to the lucky connotations of the number eight, based on the similarities in its pronunciation to the Chinese word for 'prosperity'.**

The presence of number-based superstitions cross-culturally raises the question of whether the tendency to associate numbers with auspicious and inauspicious qualities is universal. The problem is that not all societies developed numerical systems. As Thomas Crump observes in *The Anthropology of Numbers*, although numbers transcend our representations of them ($2 + 2 = 4$ is a constant, regardless of whether you have the language to describe it***), numerals—i.e., the system we use for representing

---

*Although I wonder if this effect would hold true in other locations, given that the M25 itself is widely considered to be an infernal creation—at least by anyone who's ever had the misfortune of driving on it. As Terry Pratchett and Neil Gaiman write in *Good Omens*, 'Many phenomena—wars, plagues, sudden audits—have been advanced as evidence for the hidden hand of Satan in the affairs of Man, but whenever students of demonology get together the M25 London orbital motorway is generally agreed to be among the top contenders for Exhibit A'.

**It's no coincidence that the Beijing Summer Olympics opened at 8:08:08 p.m. on the eighth day of the eighth month of 2008.

***The incontrovertibility of this fact is central to George Orwell's dystopian sci-fi novel *1984*. Resistance is fomented in the mind of Winston

numbers—are cultural creations.

Once Hindu-Arabic numerals (0, 1, 2, 3, 4, 5, 6, 7, 8, 9) came to dominate globally, these symbols permeated our lives so thoroughly that we can't see them as anything other than the numbers they represent. However, there's no intrinsic two-ness to the symbol '2'. In fact, it's far more arbitrary than the Roman numeral (II), the ancient Mayan symbol (..), and the Chinese character (二) for the same number because they visually depict the basic attributes of two itself. That Hindu-Arabic numerals came to dominate Europe in the sixteenth century is primarily due to their connection with trade and commerce, and their ease of use in the sorts of calculations and conversions required by merchants, traders, and bookkeepers.*

Numerals are a necessary precursor to arithmetic, which requires an abstract conception of numbers. According to Crump, once you have a concept of ordinal and cardinal numbers (i.e., how numbers are ordered vs how many there are in a set), their inherent divisibility is revealed, along with all sorts of intriguing properties—such as oddness and evenness, which have been producing intellectual spasms (and, I strongly suspect, orgasms**) for

---

Smith, the protagonist, when he realizes that, 'In the end the Party would announce that two plus two made five, and you would have to believe it'. The first axiom he develops in the diary where he confesses his rebellious impulses is, 'Freedom is the freedom to say that two plus two make four. If that is granted, all else follows'.

*While paper had replaced vellum in Europe, it was still a costly commodity, so the shift to Hindu-Arabic numerals made sense from a purely economic perspective, given how unwieldy Roman numerals are. To illustrate, '19,863' is 'XIXDCCCLXIII' in Roman numerals—now add a couple of thousands and imagine being a fourteenth-century bookkeeper.

**To provide an illustrative example from the sixteenth-century Paracelsian writer, Gerard Dorn, 'As one can only mate similar things with

centuries. Not all cultures developed explicit numerical systems, although implicit conceptions of numbers were often present in music and other social forms. But wherever numerical systems developed, assertions regarding the magical properties of numbers quickly followed. In *The Mystery of Numbers*, the historian Annemarie Schimmel argues that such views were underpinned by the assumption that numbers influence the character of the things that are ordered by them, thereby mediating between the natural, divine world and the one created by humans. This idea has proved remarkably persistent across time and space, reaching its epitome in the self-declared science of numerology.*

The Chinese case suggests that the magical qualities we attribute to numbers can be an unintended consequence of the symbols we use to represent them, given that a verbal coincidence is deemed responsible for the superstitions around four and eight in North Asia. This sort of representational coincidence is also used to explain the unlucky status of seventeen in Italy, which is generally attributed to its form in Roman numerals: XVII is an anagram of the Latin word 'VIXI', which translates in Latin to 'I have lived', or, less auspiciously, 'My life is over'.**

Although such assertions have the ring of convenient

---

similar things, and because God has pleasure only in odd numbers, the one unites, with its simplicity, the two into a three, and gives them a soul'.

*Despite its contemporary claims to being the 'science of self-discovery', numerology is a cultish movement that dates back to Pythagoras. Although the world has many reasons to be grateful to Pythagoras,† numerology is not one of them.

†Good luck building a stable bridge without making use of the Pythagorean Theorem.

**It's not as bad as 'guaranteed death', but Airitalia has chosen to play it safe by excluding the seat number from its planes regardless.

post-hoc explanations, there's little question that visual and aural coincidences influence the meaning we attribute to numbers. Just look at the widespread use of '69' as a euphemism to describe simultaneous acts of cunnilingus and fellatio, or the growth in idiosyncratic children's names like 'CVIIIlin', which only works if you read the middle letters as Latin numerals but pronounce them in English,* or the 1980s' children's pastime of creating 'dirty' number words on calculators.**

Whatever role such coincidences play in number superstitions, the negative and positive attributes of numbers are mostly seen to have their origins in quirks of religion and culture. A perfect illustration is the inauspicious connotations of 666:*** the number of the Beast in the Book of Revelation. Likewise, the superstition regarding the number thirteen is assumed to have biblical roots and is generally attributed to the ill-fated Last Supper, when

*My sister-in-law, a primary school teacher in a regional Australian town (the same one who taught the siblings Handsome and Princess and Shithéad and Lémon) has had a student with this name. After she overcame her confusion, my sister-in-law was too polite to point out that in the original Latin it would have been pronounced 'Coctolin', not 'Ceightlin'. But kids being kids, and Australian kids being Australian, I'm sure someone figured it out at some point, and I can guarantee that somewhere out there is a teenager who has spent most of her life saddled with the nickname 'Cock-Lint'.

**Helped by the sudden ubiquity of pocket calculators in the early 1980s, this was a popular activity when I was growing up. For example, '5318008' typed into a calculator reads 'BOOBIES' when the calculator is turned upside down—a source of great hilarity to me in primary school.

***The technical name for this is hexakosioihexekontahexaphobia. According to *Rogerson's Book of Numbers*, numerologists have had a field day with 666, insisting that the number reveals the identity of the Beast. The Roman emperor Nero is frequently deemed to be its earthly manifestation, based on numerological calculations that are too tedious (and ludicrous) to recount here.

Jesus and his disciples sat down to dine. But Jesus had twelve disciples, and the Bible suggests that they roamed all over Galilee and Jerusalem without any major calamities befalling them—unless you count the Cana wedding where they ran out of booze, forcing Jesus to turn water into wine. Focusing on that last fateful gathering as explaining the roots of the superstition is, therefore, about as valid as suggesting that the roots of the prejudice against the left hand lie in Judas's supposed sinistrality. This is probably why a secondary source for the superstition is proffered in the form of Loki's Quarrel, a story in Norse mythology in which a feast is set for twelve gods, and Loki turns up uninvited and causes trouble, precipitating the death of the god Balder.* The problem is that there are numerous accounts of the legend that vary wildly in the number of guests at the feast to the condition of Balder himself. In some stories, Balder is already dead and the feast is in his honour; in others, he dies long afterwards of unrelated events.

The fact that the number thirteen is magically charged in numerous traditions suggests that the roots of the superstition are more complex. Indeed, Schimmel notes that thirteen was widely seen to have uncanny qualities in older European folktales, but its negative attributes only came to dominate *after* the Middle Ages. Thirteen crops up in its sacred or auspicious form in the Hebrew, ancient Tibetan, Mongolian, Aztec, and Mesoamerican traditions. According to Schimmel, a common thread is the idea of thirteen

---

*If anything, the message we might take from these stories is that it's not thirteen itself but being the thirteenth person at a dinner party that's unlucky. Further support for the dinner party theory can be found in the folklorist Tok Thompson's report of a variant of *Sleeping Beauty* in which the parents have a party table set for twelve fairies; eleven arrive but a thirteenth fairy turns up in the place of the designated twelfth.

as a breakaway from the completeness of twelve—a recurring number across many traditions. The one beyond the twelve was generally either a designated leader or doomed to die (or occasionally both). Schimmel and the folklorist Tok Thompson highlight the mystical significance of thirteen in societies tracking both lunar and solar cycles, because there are 12.41 lunations per solar year. According to Schimmel, in ancient China, because of the need to periodically intercalate a thirteenth month to attune the lunar calendar to the solar year, this month was called 'Lord of Distress' or 'Lord of Oppression'. Thirteen was equally significant for the Aztecs, for whom it was a sacred number. There were thirteen heavens, thirteen solar years was the age when a boy became a man, fifty-two (13 × 4) was regarded as the end of adulthood and beginning of old age, and there were 676 years (13 × 52) in a 'sun' or era.

The same is true of other symbolically charged numbers in the Western tradition, such as seven and three. Throughout much of the world, seven has lucky associations, seeming to obtain its allure from a variety of disparate sources: Christianity, Islam, Judaism, and Buddhism, but also the ancient Babylonians, Sumerians, and Mayans. Notably, God created the world in seven days, there are seven notes on a music scale, as well as Seven Wonders of the World, seven seas, and seven celestial bodies circling the Earth (well, until Copernicus suggested otherwise). Three likewise crops up repeatedly across various mythologies; for example, many religious traditions feature versions of the Trinity. Good things happen in threes: wishes, charms, wise men. But then, so do bad things. Goldilocks incurred the wrath of three bears, the wolf tried to knock down the houses of three pigs, and it was three, not four, witches Macbeth met on the moor. The same goes for seven. If you break a mirror, you have seven years of bad luck; couples get the seven-year itch, there are seven deadly sins, and so on. Significantly, these dual attributes are also widely found outside Western traditions, suggesting that all three numbers (three, seven, and thirteen) can have a positive or negative valence depending on the context.

But that's not the only commonality they share—they are all odd numbers, but, more significantly, they are all *prime* numbers, i.e., numbers that are not divisible, except by one, itself a prime. Odd numbers have often been associated with peculiar powers—something evident in their name.* According to Schimmel, a key doctrine of the Pythagoreans was that even numbers were associated with the left, inferior, female side, whilst odd numbers were the province of the right, superior, masculine side. But primes are special types of odd numbers because they refuse to be divided at all;** furthermore, they are unpredictable. As the mathematician Matthew Watkins observes, primes have long posed a mathematical quandary because they are seemingly randomly distributed. It therefore makes sense that anomalous numbers are more likely to be symbolically charged with powerful and potentially polluting qualities. Because they don't fit normal numerical rules and patterns, they epitomize 'matter out of place' in Mary Douglas's sense of the term. This suggests that while the roots of our fixation with numbers are primarily cultural, their natural properties have a role to play in which ones

---

*The etymology of the word 'odd' comes from the Old Norse and meant 'constituting a unit in excess of an even number'; the sense of 'strange, peculiar' emerged in the late sixteenth century.

**Although prime numbers have a unique status in many numerical systems, seven has a distinct status amongst primes, because it's the only number between one and ten that doesn't produce other numbers in the set when doubled, unlike the other primes. This is the sort of thing that throws numerologists into paroxysms of delight.

are deemed significant. Indeed, in number theory, numbers are described as 'happy', 'evil', and 'odious' based on their distinctive attributes in mathematical operations.

But why are we so prone to attributing qualities to numbers beyond their role in quantification? As Matthew Watkins observes, 'There's a huge gulf between the dominant "scientific" (that is, quantitative) approach to numbers and the qualitative "folk beliefs" regarding numbers'. While the unusual attributes of numbers like three, seven, and thirteen help explain how they became so prominent in cross-cultural superstitions, it doesn't tell us why. Many observers explain this by reference to the concept of 'magical thinking'—which is typically used to mean the erroneous belief that one's individual actions can influence events in the material world. Superstitions of all kinds, especially those relating to numbers, are often dismissed as evidence of magical thinking.* For example, in *Fooled by Randomness: The Hidden Role of Chance in Markets and Life*, the statistician Nassim Nicholas Taleb compares contemporary superstitions to 'some primitive tribesman [who] scratched his nose, saw rain falling, and developed an elaborate method of scratching his nose to bring on the much-needed rain'.

This negative view of magical thinking has its roots in the work of the nineteenth-century anthropologist Sir James Frazer, who argued that magic was a parallel, albeit inferior, system to science. According to Frazer, magical systems of thought assumed that the succession of events was determined by immutable laws, but, unlike science, they misconceived these laws through a series of mistaken

---

*'Magical thinking' has pejorative connotations. This is partly because of the ways that psychologists have hijacked the term to describe pathological behaviours—such as the frequent number fixations amongst people suffering from obsessive-compulsive disorder.

associations. Frazer therefore insisted that magic was science's 'bastard sister'.* But Frazer's ideas and those of his contemporaries were soon superseded by the subsequent generation of anthropologists who conducted fieldwork in societies where magical beliefs were commonplace. For example, based on his extended fieldwork in the Trobriand Islands (an archipelago of coral atolls off the east coast of Papua New Guinea), Bronislaw Malinowski argued that magical and practical work in the realms of farming and fishing generally went together, but this didn't mean that the islanders confused magic and science. Magic, he argued, was only employed in contexts where there was an element of chance and uncertainty in the outcome. In Malinowski's view, magic was, therefore, a functional response to uncertainty, and magical rituals were limited to contexts where rational techniques couldn't be relied upon to produce a certain outcome.

Nassim Nicholas Taleb aside, Malinowki's more congenial analysis of magical thinking is commonly drawn on in accounts of number superstitions. In *Quirkology: The Curious Science of Everyday Lives*, Richard Wiseman makes recourse to Malinowksi's view of magic as providing 'a sense of control over the slings and arrows of outrageous fortune', suggesting that the same pattern underlies contemporary superstitions around numbers and objects. The anthropologist George Gmelch has been similarly inspired by Malinowski in his research on baseball magic. As Gmelch illustrates, number superstitions are rife amongst American professional baseballers, from rituals such as arising at exactly 10 a.m. on match day and tapping the home plate

---

*The Golden Bough was written in 1890, when 'bastard' was still the technical term for an illegitimate child. It was only in the twentieth century that it became widely used as a swear word. This is a good example of orthophemistic (descriptive) rather than dysphemistic (offensive) usage.

three times before batting, to the special significance many baseballers place on their uniform number. According to Gmelch, when Ricky Henderson arrived at the Blue Jays in 1993, he paid outfielder Turner Ward $25,000 for the right to wear number twenty-four. Gmelch argues, 'Since their livelihoods depend on how well they perform, many use magic to try and control the chance that is built into baseball', which is why superstitions are most prominent in those parts of the game that are more dependent on factors that players can't personally control—such as pitching and hitting, rather than fielding.

Ample evidence of similar number superstitions can be found across many professional sports. When Michael Jordan joined the Chicago Bulls, number twenty-three became globally famous following his sponsorship deal with Nike, and Jordan's meteoric rise as a basketball player. As the series *The Last Dance* documents, upon his return to the NBA in 1995 following a stint in minor league baseball, Jordan initially played under his baseball number (forty-five) but swiftly reverted to twenty-three after Orlando Magic player Nick Anderson observed that 'number forty-five is not number twenty-three'—and, indeed, Jordan's performance markedly improved after the switch.

A similar conflation between man and number is evident in Cristiano Ronaldo's association with the number seven—now immortalized in his global CR7 brand.* It was

---

*That said, Ronaldo hasn't been able to claim ownership over the number in popular culture in the same way that Jordan has been able to claim twenty-three (a prime number, I note), there being too much competition from other sources. His cultural stature is such that he can almost compete with James Bond (a.k.a. 007). But while he has inspired an extraordinary volume of bad poetry, he can't really hold a candle to the Seven Wonders of the World, despite his superb form (he's a pretty

Manchester United's manager, Sir Alex Ferguson, who convinced Ronaldo to take 'lucky' number seven, which had previously been worn by other United football greats, and Ronaldo's success at United soon solidified the association. When Ronaldo moved to Real Madrid in 2009, he had to wait for a year before he could reclaim the number seven, but when he moved to Juventus in Italy, Ronaldo negotiated the number seven jersey, which he took from a teammate upon arrival. The same happened with his return to Manchester United, which saw him reclaim the number seven jersey from his teammate Edinson Cavani, who then reverted to twenty-one—the number Cavani uses when he plays for his home country Uruguay. Again and again, we see the same pattern: jersey numbers are never just numbers for players, or at least not for long.

The distinct relationship between humans and numbers is best summed up in Honoré de Balzac's observation that, 'Numbers are intellectual witnesses that belong only to mankind'. However, the testimony they give isn't always reliable. Take 7734206. Some people might see an inauspicious number (4) surrounded by innocuous siblings, or a pattern in which the beginning and end numbers equal the sum of the middle number and its left and right counterpart, respectively. Others, typing it into their pocket calculator and turning it upside down, might see it as a hidden message ('90ᴧhELL'). Others, still, may assume it reveals the location of a portal to Hell itself (based on international postal codes, that would be Rambam 10 in Ashdod, Israel).

The point is that if you look long enough, you'll start to see patterns *because that's what humans do*. While number superstitions may be a functional means of managing uncer-

---

good footballer too).

tainty, this assumes they are a by-product of our inability to cope with randomness—a fault in our wiring that demonstrates the limits of our rationality. But everything that makes us human relies on our capacity for recognizing patterns and making connections; this isn't something that we can just switch on and off at will, like a light. In fact, if we managed to get the switch off, we'd never get it back on because we would have forgotten what a switch is! In the end, if it's a matter of keeping the lights on (literally and metaphorically), well, what's a little triskaidekaphobia between friends?

Conclusion

As we have come to the end of our time together, you will naturally (albeit optimistically*) expect me to close with some incisive reflections on the central messages of this book. Having perused various bestsellers for inspiration, it's clear that there are two distinct genres of conclusion for works of this kind. While some authors prefer the enumerated list outlining the book's core insights, others conclude with a story or anecdote that supposedly conveys the same thing, without the author having to do anything as passé as sum things up.** In the interests of maximizing my chances of presenting something that resembles a conclusion, I offer three closing thoughts *and* a story.

First, there is clearly a logic to our beliefs and be-

---

*I assume it's by now abundantly clear that wrapping things up is not my strong point.† Still, as Ralph Waldo Emerson once said, it's the journey, not the destination, that counts (although he was, of course, was talking about life rather than books).

†Unless you haven't actually read the book but are considering buying it, in which case I'm only joking.

**These are often labelled as an 'epilogue', which seems to be code for 'I couldn't be arsed writing a proper conclusion'.

haviours, although it often takes a distinctively cultural form. As Gillian Tett observes in *Anthro-Vision*, 'we must accept that there is no single "natural" cultural frame'. Thus, the meaning of white teeth, toilet paper, body odour, and buying rounds, along with the most appropriate location for the washing machine, differ as you cross countries—even ones we consider to be broadly similar. Some ideas and practices do seem to transcend culture, speaking to certain underlying patterns in human thought that are potentially influenced by biology and evolution. But even these patterns tend to be culturally inflected: the extent to which the left hand is devalued, the linguistic differences in what constitutes swearing, and the polluting qualities attributed to 'matter out of place' are cases in point.

Second, we think primarily in metaphors. We understand humans via the lens of animals and animals via the lens of humans. We use our bodies as a model for society and nature as a model for our bodies. Objects likewise become symbolic of social relations. In consequence, nothing ever stays in its place: not animals, not farts, not gifts, or the left hand, and certainly not numbers. You imagine otherwise at your peril—like poor Steve, whose unrepented fart was taken as an act of aggression, or my unsuccessful attempts to convince Koreans that my left-handedness was not a sign of my foreignness, or anyone who has ever been fooled by the words 'free gift'.

Third, and probably most importantly, we lie to ourselves *constantly*—from why we obsess over our teeth and tip waitstaff to where we place our home appliances and whether gifts need to be reciprocated. This is why anthropologists quickly learn to focus on what people do rather than what they say—or, as Malcolm Gladwell calls it, 'listening with your eyes'.* In sum, almost everything we say about everything we do, no matter how plausible it sounds, should be taken with a grain of salt. As I've shown throughout this book, you can pretty much guarantee that any so-called factual origin story for our beliefs or behaviours is wishful thinking at best.

Consider the expression 'take it with a grain of salt' itself. Most online sources blithely declare that its origins lie in eating practices in antiquity, and the view that food was more easily swallowed with a small amount of salt. A variant on this line of argument attributes the phrase to the Roman philosopher Pliny the Elder, who described an antidote to poison in his book *Naturalis Historia* that included 'the addition of a grain of salt'. Thus, even the declared origins of the expression 'take it with a grain of salt' should be taken with a grain of salt.

But it's not a surprise that salt crops up so frequently in our language. A staple in every settled society on record, salt has frequently been accorded the status of the 'Fifth Element', alongside air, water, fire, and earth. The cultural significance of salt is reflected in numerous Latin words. *Salus* and *salubris*, the respective Latin terms for 'health' and 'healthy', derive from it, which explains the roots of the English word 'salubrious'. 'Salary' likewise comes from *salarium*, which is frequently (albeit questionably) said to derive from the ancient Roman practice of paying soldiers in salt.** Its appearance isn't limited to European contexts either. For example, Brazilians use the expression *'Sem sal sem açúcar'* (literally 'without salt, without sugar') to de-

*This expression has the advantage of sounding pithy and profound, while making basically no sense.

**As historical evidence to support this explanation is lacking, the story about Roman soldiers being paid in grains (or at least grams) of salt should be taken with, you guessed it, a grain of salt.

scribe something that is lacklustre or dull. In Korean, the expression *jjeonda*, which translates as 'awesome', 'cool', or 'dope' in English, seems to be etymologically connected with the term for pickling something in salt or sugar.

Salt's cultural meanings clearly stem from its physiological significance, which is alluded to in both the Brazilian and Korean expressions. The taste for salt is universal and shared by many of our non-human relatives; it is also essential for food storage and preservation. The story of salt, as the historian Samuel Adshead has illustrated, is the story of human civilization. Salt was critical to the rise of trade and commerce, and the globalization of food commodity chains. It also played a role in our ability to harness energy—the first true battery, created by the Italian physicist Alessandro Volta in 1800, involved copper, zinc, water, and salt. The point is that even a seemingly insignificant substance like salt enables us to, in the words of the anthropologist Sidney Mintz, 'unearth anew the history of ourselves'.

As I have hopefully demonstrated throughout this book, virtually any topic, no matter how mundane (or low-brow), potentially offers insights into what it means to be human. In fact, surely those are the best subjects to study, because it's often the little things that turn out to be the most revealing—just like an unconscious 'tell' in a poker game that gives an observant player insight into the hand another holds.

This isn't to say that anthropologists have always been willing to turn our gaze towards such phenomena—we are no less immune to cultural blind spots than anyone else. But as Tett illustrates, you don't need to be an anthropologist to think anthropologically. Ultimately, anthro-vision draws attention to our taken-for-granted beliefs and behaviours and asks us to move beyond common-sense explanations for why we do the things we do. Whether it be why we tend to conflate food and sex or what makes a joke funny, the answers to such questions tell us something useful about ourselves—although to learn more about those, you'll have to wait for the next book.*

---

*This implies that a second book is in the offing. The 1980s film *Mac & Me* is a good illustration of the dangers of this sort of over-confidence. A spectacularly bad†—and blatantly derivative—rip-off of *E.T.*, a sequel was planned from the outset, with viewers told at the end of the film to keep an eye out for the forthcoming sequel (I guess the producers figured that anyone who made it the whole way through was undiscriminating enough to pay for a repeat of the experience). The abysmal box office performance of *Mac & Me* ensured that *Mac & Me II* was never made. Only time will tell as to whether this book is the literary equivalent of *Mac & Me*.

†This movie is so bad that my siblings and I used it as our bar for bad movies for the remainder of our childhoods.

Sources

PREFACE

Fox, Kate. 2014. *Watching the English.* Second Edition. Hodder & Stoughton.

Geertz, Clifford. 1973. *The Interpretation of Cultures.* Basic Books.

Tett, Gillian. 2021. *Anthro-Vision: How Anthropology Can Explain Business and Life.* Penguin Random House.

1. SILENT BUT DEADLY

Ackerman, Diane. 1991. *A Natural History of the Senses.* Vintage Books.

Allen, Valerie. 2007. *On Farting: Language and Laughter in the Middle Ages.* Palgrave Macmillan.

BBC News. 2019. Fart bullying case: Engineer contests A$1.8m court ruling. *BBC News,* 26 March. https://www.bbc.co.uk/news/world-australia-47702527

Classen, Constance, David Howe, and Anthony Synnott. 2002. *Aroma: The Cultural History of Smell.* Routledge.

Carballo, Charlie. 2014. 'I did NOT fart on air!': Whoopi Goldberg insists flatulence noise in The View was a 'sound effect' she turned into a joke. *Mail Online,* 12 December. https://www.dailymail.co.uk/tvshowbiz/

article-2871704/Whoopi-Goldberg-insists-flatulence-noise-View-sound-effect-turned-joke.html

Crocker, Jon. 1985. *Vital Souls: Bororo Cosmology, Natural Symbolism, and Shamanism.* University of Arizona Press.

Douglas, Mary. 2003. *Purity and Danger: An Analysis of the Concepts of Pollution and Taboo.* Routledge.

Douglas, Leonard & Garvey. 2021. Is farting in the workplace a form of bullying? *Douglas, Leonard & Garvey Blog*, P.C., 5 July. https://www.nhlawoffice.com/blog/2021/july/is-farting-in-the-workplace-a-form-of-bullying-/

Elias, Norbert. 1994. *The Civilizing Process: Sociogenetic and Psychogenetic Investigations.* Translated by Edmund Jephcott. Revised Edition. Blackwell Publishing.

Jack Vale Films. 2013. Punched for farting (extended, raw). *YouTube*, October 26. https://www.youtube.com/watch?v=ATqC3Lgm-js&t=74s

Jack Vale Films. 2011. Old man farting returns! *YouTube*, October 13. https://www.youtube.com/watch?v=YM-JPrNQxPNA

Kristeva, Julia. 1982. *Powers of Horror: An Essay on Abjection.* Columbia University Press.

McGuire, Caroline. 2017. Hot air plane: Flight attendants fart on planes by pretending to perform aisle checks… and they call it 'crop dusting'. *The Sun*, 29 March. https://www.thesun.co.uk/travel/3381319/flight-attendants-fart-crop-dusting-planes/

Muir, Frank. 1983. *An Irreverent and Almost Complete Social History of the Bathroom.* Stein & Day.

Price, K.R., J. Lewis, G.M. Wyatt, and G.R. Fenwick. 1988. Review article: Flatulence—Causes, relation to diet and remedies. *Molecular Nutrition & Food Research*, 32(6): 609–626.

Seeger, Anthony. 1988. Anthropology and odor: From Manhattan to Mato Grosso. *Perfumer & Flavorist*, 13: 41–48.

Thomas, Nicholas. 2015. A critique of the natural artefact: Anthropology, art & museology. *Art History Lecture Series* 13. https://www.repository.cam.ac.uk/handle/1810/254833

Wen, Lily. 2000. Colonialism, gender and work: A voice from the People of the Lily and the Leopard. *Anthropology of Work Review*, 21(3): 24–27.

Westermarck, Edward. 2014. *Ritual and Belief in Morocco.* Volumes I and II. Routledge.

2. PITS OF DESPAIR

Ackerman, Diane. 1990. *A Natural History of the Senses.* Random House.

Carpenter, Edmund. 1973. *Eskimo Realities.* Holt, Rinehart & Winston.

Classen, Constance. 1992. The odour of the other: Olfactory symbolism and cultural categories. *Ethos*, 20(2): 133–166.

Classen, Constance, David Howes, and Anthony Synnott. 1994. *Aroma: The Cultural History of Smell.* Routledge.

Corbin, Alain. 1994. *The Foul and the Fragrant: Odour and the Social Imagination.* Picador.

Dental Depot. 2018. The surprising history of halitosis. *Dental Depot*, 7 December. https://dentaldepot.net/history-of-halitosis/

Dick, Philip K. 2016. The chromium fence. In *The Philip K. Dick Reader.* Citadel Press.

Elias, Norbert. 1994. *The Civilizing Process: Sociogenetic and Psychogenetic Investigations.* Translated by Edmund Jephcott. Revised Edition. Blackwell Publishing.

Eng, Julie. 2013. You'll smell better: 7 unusual reasons to go veg. *Sierra: The Magazine of the Sierra Club*, 7 October. https://www.sierraclub.org/sierra/2013-5-september-october/green-life/youll-smell-better-7-unusual-reasons-go-veg

Freud, Sigmund. 2014. *Civilization and Its Discontents.* Penguin Classics.

Guo, Owen. 2018. Aiming at China's armpits: When foreign brands misfire. *New York Times*, 2 February. https://www.nytimes.com/2018/02/02/business/china-consumers-deodorant.html

Havlicek, Jan and Pavlina Lenochova. 2006. The effect of meat consumption on body odor attractiveness. *Chemical Senses*, 31(8): 747–752.

Khanna, Kanika. 2021. Microbial origins of body odor. *American Society for Microbiology*, 30 December. https://asm.org/Articles/2021/December/Microbial-Origins-of-Body-Odor

Labows, J.N. and Preti, G. 1992. Human semiochemicals. In *Fragrance: The Psychology and Biology of Perfume*, edited by S. Van Toller and G.H. Dodd. Kluwer, pp. 69-90.

Le Guérer, Annick. 1990. *Scent: The Essential and Mysterious Powers of Smell.* Kodansha International.

Levis-Strauss, Claude. 1973. *From Honey to Ashes.* Harper & Row.

MacPhee, Marybeth. 1992. Deodorized culture: Anthropology of smell in America. *Arizona Anthropologist*, 8: 89–102.

Orwell, George. 2021. *The Road to Wigan Pier.* Oxford University Press.

Searing, Bryan. 2018. From sinking product to $1B gem. *Medium*, 1 January. https://medium.com/swlh/from-sinking-product-to-1b-gem-c953725652ca

Stoddart, D. Michael. 1990. *The Scented Ape: The Biology and Culture of Human Odour.* Cambridge University Press.

Yuhas, Daisy. 2014. Are human pheromones real? *Scientific American*, 1 May. https://www.scientificamerican.com/article/are-human-pheromones-real/

Zuniga, Andrea, Richard J. Stevenson, Mehmut K. Mahmut, and Ian D. Stephen. 2017. Diet quality and the attractiveness of male body odor. *Evolution & Human Behavior*, 38: 136–143.

3. FOR THE LOVE OF TOILET PAPER

Baddeley, Michelle. 2020. Toilet paper mania. *Psychology Today*, 8 March. https://www.psychologytoday.com/us/blog/copycats-and-contrarians/202003/toilet-paper-mania

Bellalyn. 2020. Langley Costco panic buying 'toilet paper race' | This is insane!!! *YouTube*, 9 March. https://www.youtube.com/watch?v=kfxETe8uKbw

Chilton, Brian G. 2018. Reference guide to the biblical symbolism of colors. *Crossexamined.org*, 5 February. https://crossexamined.org/reference-guide-to-the-biblical-symbolism-of-colors/

Douglas, Mary. 2003. *Purity and Danger: An Analysis of the Concepts of Pollution and Taboo.* Routledge.

Garbe, Lisa, Richard Rau, and Theo Toppe. 2020. Influence of perceived threat of Covid-19 and HEACO personality traits on toilet paper stockpiling. *PLoS ONE*, 15(6): e0234232.

Inglis, David. 2001. *A Sociological History of Excretory Experience: Defecatory Manners and Toiletry Technologies.* Edwin Mellon Press.

Malcolm, Andrew H. 1974. The 'shortage' of bathroom tissue: Classic study in rumor. *New York Times*, 3 February. https://www.nytimes.com/1974/02/03/archives/the-shortage-of-bathroom-tissue-a-classic-study-in-rumor-shortage.html

Nash, Stephen E. 2018. What did ancient Romans do without toilet paper? *Sapiens*, 3 April. https://www.sapiens.org/column/curiosities/ancient-roman-bathrooms/

Otsuki, Grant Jun. 2020. Shit's getting real: A cultural analysis of toilet paper. *Grant Jun Otsuki: Anthropology of Science, Technology, and Japan*, 11 March. https://www.gjotsuki.net/shits-getting-real-a-cultural-analysis-of-toilet-paper

Paloyo, Alfredo. 2020. A toilet paper run is like a bank run. The economic fixes are about the same. *The Conversation,* 6 March. https://theconversation.com/a-toilet-paper-run-is-like-a-bank-run-the-economic-fixes-are-about-the-same-133065

Praeger, Dave. 2007. *Poop Culture: How America is Shaped by Its Grossest National Product.* Feral House.

Rosner, Helen. 2020. We are all irrational panic shoppers. *The New Yorker,* 5 March. https://www.newyorker.com/culture/annals-of-gastronomy/we-are-all-irrational-panic-shoppers

Samarajiva, Indi. 2019. White people, you need to wash your butts. *Medium,* 11 July. https://indica.medium.com/white-people-you-need-to-wash-your-butts-a1dd-1a1b2bef

Siniawer, Eiko Murko. 2018. *Waste: Consuming Postwar Japan.* Cornell University Press.

Smith, Richard. 2012. *Bum Fodder: An Absorbing History of Toilet Paper.* Souvenir Press.

Stratton, Jon. 2021. Coronavirus, the great toilet paper panic and civilisation. *Thesis Eleven,* 165(1): 145–168.

The Japan Times. 2020. Toto posts brisk sales in bidet toilets in U.S. in fiscal 2020. *The Japan Times,* 29 April. https://www.japantimes.co.jp/news/2021/04/29/business/corporate-business/toto-toilet-north-america/

Turner, Victor W. 1966. Colour classification in Ndembu ritual. In *Anthropological Approaches to the Study of Religion,* edited by Michael Banton. Cornell University Press, pp. 59–92.

9 News Australia. 2020. Shoppers charged over toilet paper brawl. *YouTube,* 8 March. https://www.youtube.com/watch?v=Y1nEnOmC6IQ

Doomsday. 2020. Crazy toilet paper panic buying UK Coronavirus Covid-19. *YouTube Shorts.* https://www.youtube.com/shorts/-6nP-1Igrb0

Wieczner, Jen. The case of the missing toilet paper: How

the coronavirus exposed U.S. supply chain flaws. *Fortune*, 18 May. https://fortune.com/2020/05/18/toilet-paper-sales-surge-shortage-coronavirus-pandemic-supply-chain-cpg-panic-buying/

4. GOING TO THE DENTIST BITES

Bailit, Howard L. 1968. A possible benefit from tooth-blackening. *American Anthropologist*, 70(2): 348–353.

Closer Staff. 2021. Tom Cruise has one of Hollywood's most famous smiles! See the story behind the actor's 'middle tooth'. *Closer Weekly*, 19 April. https://www.closerweekly.com/posts/tom-cruise-middle-tooth-138120/

Frazer, James G. 2013. *The Golden Bough*. Third Edition. Cambridge University Press.

Handwerker, W. Penn and Stanton H. Wolf. 2010. Where bad teeth come from: Culture and causal force. *Human Organization*, 69(4): 398–406.

Hueston, Dave. 2020. Orthodontist setting Japan straight on teeth. *Kyodo News*, 16 January. https://english.kyodonews.net/news/2020/01/d6607201f341-feature-orthodontist-setting-japan-straight-on-teeth.html

Khalid, Abeer and Carlos Quiñonez. 2015. Straight, white teeth as a social prerogative. *Sociology of Health & Illness*, 37(5): 782–976.

Larson, Rebecca. 2017. Queen Elizabeth's rotten teeth. *Tudors Dynasty*, 13 December. https://tudorsdynasty.com/queen-elizabeths-rotten-teeth/

Linn, Erwin L. 1966. Social meanings of dental appearance. *Journal of Health & Human Behavior*, 7(4): 289–295.

Miner, Horace. 1956. Body ritual among the Nacirema. *American Anthropologist*, 58(3): 503–507.

Sedaris, David. 2020. Dentists without borders. In *The Best of Me*. Abacus.

Shulman, Jay D., Gerardo Maupomé, D. Christopher

Clark, and Steven M. Levy. 2004. Perceptions of desirable tooth color amongst parents, dentists and children. *Journal of the American Dental Association*, 135: 595–604.

Simonitch, Steven. 2013. Why Japanese women go for fake crooked teeth. *Japan Today*, 31 January. https://japantoday.com/category/features/lifestyle/why-japa-nese-women-go-for-fake-crooked-teeth

Slack, Maura E., Edward J. Swift, Jr, P. Emile Rossouw, and Ceib Phillips. 2013. Tooth whitening in the orthodontic practice: A survey of orthodontists. *American Journal of Orthodontics & Dentofacial Orthopedics*, 143(4): S64–S71.

Tuleja, Tad. 1991. The Tooth Fairy: Perspectives on money and magic. In *The Good People: New Fairylore Essays*, edited by Peter Narváez. University Press of Kentucky, pp. 406–424.

Wells, Rosemary. 1991. The making of an icon: The Tooth Fairy in North American folklore and popular culture. In *The Good People: New Fairylore Essays*, edited by Peter Narváez. University Press of Kentucky, pp. 426–454.

Zumbroich, Thomas J. 2011. To strengthen the teeth and harden the gums—teeth blackening as medical practice in Asia, Micronesia and Melanesia. *Ethnobotany Research & Applications*, 9: 97–113.

Zumbroich, Thomas. 2015. 'We blacken our teeth with oko to make them firm': Teeth blackening in Oceania. *Anthropologica*, 57(2): 539–555.

Zumbroich, Thomas and Analyn Salvador-Amores. 2009. 'When black teeth were beautiful'—the history and ethnography of dental modifications in Luzon, Philippines. *Stvdia Asiatica*, X: 125–165.

5. LAUNDRY LOCATION, LOCATION, LOCATION

Attfield, Judy. 1999. Bringing modernity home: Open plan in the British domestic interior. In *At Home: An Anthropology of Domestic Space*, edited by Irene Cieraad. Syracuse University Press, pp. 1–12.

Attfield, Judy. 2007. *Bringing Modernity Home: Writings on Popular Design and Material Culture.* Manchester University Press.

Broderick, Ryan. 2017. It's time to accept that British people are right, your washing machine should be in the kitchen. *BuzzFeed News*, 14 July. https://www.buzzfeednews.com/article/ryanhatesthis/its-time-to-accept-that-british-people-are-right-your

Bryson, Bill. 2000. *In a Sunburned Country.* Broadway Books.

Cieraad, Irene, editor. 1999. Introduction: Anthropology at home. In *At Home: An Anthropology of Domestic Space.* Syracuse University Press, pp. 1–12.

DecoAlert. 2021. Answer: What do the British call a living room? *DecoAlert*, 6 July. https://decoalert.com/answer-what-do-the-british-call-a-living-room/

Douglas, Mary. 2003. *Purity and Danger: An Analysis of the Concepts of Pollution and Taboo.* Routledge.

Fox, Kate. 2014. *Watching the English.* Second Edition. Hodder & Stoughton.

Freeman, Hadley. 2017. Washed up: Kirstie Allsopp's kitchen-stink drama. *The Guardian*, 13 July. https://www.theguardian.com/lifeandstyle/lostinshowbiz/2017/jul/13/washed-up-kirstie-allsopps-kitchen-stink-drama?CMP=gu_com

Furseth, Jessica. 2017. Our fridges, ourselves. *Curbed*, 19 July. https://archive.curbed.com/2017/7/19/15915268/using-us-uk-electrical-appliances-american-home-tech

Hand, Martin, Elizabeth Shove, and Dale Southerton. 2007. Home extensions in the United Kingdom: Space, time, and practice. *Environment & Planning D:*

Society & Space, 25(4): 668–681.

Hartley-Brewer, Julia. 2017. A posh flat, a holiday cottage, a mansion staffed by six... welcome to the wonky world of Kirstie Allsnob. *The Sun*, 13 July. https://www.thesun.co.uk/news/4006714/a-posh-flat-a-holiday-cottage-a-mansion-staffed-by-six-welcome-to-the-world-of-kirstie-allsnob/

Johnson, Louise C. 2006. Browsing the modern kitchen—a feast of gender, place and culture (Part 1). *Gender, Place & Culture*, 13(2): 123–132.

Kelly, Tamara. 2020. Is it the end of open-plan living? New findings reveal a new lifestyle trend proving more popular. *Ideal Home*, 24 September. https://www.idealhome.co.uk/news/new-lifestyle-trend-more-popular-than-open-plan-living-255500

Point2Homes. 2017. Home sizes in the US: Expectations vs reality. *Point2homes.com*, 10 February. https://www.point2homes.com/news/us-real-estate-news/home-sizes-expectations-reality.html

Purtill, Corinne. 2017. One household staple sums up why Americans and Brits will never see the world in the same way. *Quartz*, 21 July. https://qz.com/1034914/it-doesnt-matter-where-brits-keep-their-dryers-the-point-is-they-dont-work/

Vincent, Tanya. 2005. New world order. *The Guardian*, 13 August. https://www.theguardian.com/money/2005/aug/13/property.homesandgardens

YouGov. 2017. Location, Location, Location host Kirstie Allsopp has come under fire for agreeing with a view attributed to American workers in London that the British habit of putting washing machines in kitchens is 'disgusting'. *YouGov*, 12 July. https://yougov.co.uk/topics/lifestyle/survey-results/daily/2017/07/12/53410/1

6. A SLUG IS A SNAIL WITHOUT A HOUSE

Bowker, Geoffrey and Susan Leigh Star 2000. *Sorting Things Out: Classification and Its Consequences.* MIT Press.

Bulmer, Ralph. 1967. Why is the cassowary not a bird? A problem of zoological taxonomy among the Karam of the New Guinea Highlands. *Man NS*, 2(1): 5–25.

Bulmer, Ralph. 1970. Which came first? The chicken or the egg-head? *Studies in General Anthropology.* Volume II. Échanges et Communications: Mélanges Offerts a Claude Lévi-Strauss, edited Jean Pouillon and Pierre Maranda. Mouton, pp. 1069-1091.

Diamond, Jared. 1988. *Guns, Germs and Steel: A Short History of Everybody for the Last 13,000 Years.* Vintage.

Durkheim, Émile and Marcel Mauss. 1963. *Primitive Classification.* Translated by Rodney Needman. Cohen & West.

Dwyer, Peter, D. 2005. Ethnoclassification, ethnoecology and the imagination. *Journal de la Sociétié des Océanistes*, 120–121.

Encyclopaedia Britannica. 2022. Snail and slug. *Kids. Britannica.com.* https://kids.britannica.com/kids/article/snail-and-slug/353784#:~:text=Snails%20and%20slugs%20are%20similar,oysters%2C%20clams%2C%20and%20squid.

Eom, Young-Ho, Pablo Aragón, David Lanciado, Andreas Kaltenbrunner, Sebastiano Vigna, and Dima L. Shep-elyansky. 2015. Interaction of cultures and top people of Wikipedia from ranking of 24 language editions. *PLoS One*, 10(3): e0114825.

Etymologeek. 2022. Limace etymology. https://etymolo-geek.com/fra/limace

Fara, Patricia. 2004. *Sex, Botany and Empire: The Story of Carl Linnaeus and Joseph Banks.* Columbia University Press.

Fernandez-Armesto, Felipe. 2002. *Near a Thousand Tables: A History of Food.* Free Press.

Foucault, Michel. 2005. *The Order of Things.* Routledge.

George, Sam. 2005. 'Not strictly proper for a female pen': Eighteenth-century poetry and the sexuality of botany. *Comparative Critical Studies*, 2(2): 67–91.

Gribbon, Mary and John Gribbon. 2008. *Flower Hunters.* Oxford University Press.

Groves, C.P. 2017. The latest thinking about the taxonomy of great apes. *International Zoo Yearbook*, 52(1): 16–24.

Harrison, Peter. 2009. Linnaeus as a second Adam? Taxonomy and the religious vocation. *Zygon*, 44(4): 879–893.

Leach, Edmund. 1989. Anthropological aspects of language: Animal categories and verbal abuse. *Anthrozoös*, 2(3): 151–165.

Lévi-Strauss, Claude. 1962. *The Savage Mind.* University of Chicago Press.

McNulty, Kieran P. 2016. Hominin taxonomy and phylogeny: What's in a name? *Nature Education Knowledge*, 7(1): 2.

Harper, Douglas. 2022. Escargot. *Online Etymology Dictionary.* https://www.etymonline.com/word/escargot

Harper, Douglas. 2022. Slug. *Online Etymology Dictionary.* https://www.etymonline.com/word/slug

Harper, Douglas. 2022. Snail. *Online Etymology Dictionary.* https://www.etymonline.com/word/snail#etymonline_v_23754

Moore, Randy. 1997. Linnaeus and the sexual lives of plants. *The American Biology Teacher*, 59(3): 132.

Pearce, Timothy A. 2020. What's so good about being a slug? *Carnegie Museum of Natural History.* https://carnegiemnh.org/whats-so-good-about-being-a-slug/#:~:text=Slugs%20evolved%20from%20snails%20by,multilineata%20from%20Ann%20Arbor%2C%20Michigan.

University of Nebraska-Lincoln State Museum Division of Entomology. 2022. Carl Linnaeus 1707-1778. *Scarab Workers World Directory.* https://unsm-ento.unl.edu/workers/CLinnaeus.htm

Schiebinger, Londa. 1993. Why mammals are called mammals: Gender politics in eighteenth-century natural history. *The American Historical Review*, 98(2): 382–411.

The Snail Wrangler. 2022. Frequently Asked Questions. http://www.thesnailwrangler.com

7. MUST LOVE DOGS

Amazon. 2019. Meet the dogs of Amazon. *Amazon Blog*, 30 July. https://www.aboutamazon.com/news/workplace/how-much-does-amazon-love-dogs-just-ask-one-of-the-7-000-pups-that-work-here

BBC News. 2020. US ends era of emotional support animals on planes. *BBC News*, 3 December. https://www.bbc.co.uk/news/world-us-canada-55177736

Coren, Stanley. 2006. *The Intelligence of Dogs.* Atria Books.

Donaldson James, Susan. 2011. Leona Helmsley's little rich dog Trouble dies in luxury. *ABC News*, 10 June. https://abcnews.go.com/US/leona-helmsleys-dog-trouble-richest-world-dies-12/story?id=13810168

Eschner, Kate. 2017. Mark Twain liked cats better than people. *Smithsonian Magazine*, 16 October. https://www.smithsonianmag.com/smart-news/mark-twain-liked-cats-better-people-180965265/

Freud Museum London. 2019. Was Freud more of a dog person than a cat person? *Freud Museum Blog*, 14 October. https://www.freud.org.uk/2019/10/14/was-freud-more-of-a-dog-person-than-a-cat-person/

Freud, Sigmund. 2014. *Civilization and Its Discontents.* Penguin Classics.

Haraway, Donna. 2008. *When Species Meet.* University of Minnesota Press.

Hills, Megan, C. 2019. Dog and cat Instagram influencers estimated to earn as much as $32k for a single sponsored post. *Evening Standard*, 19 December. https://www.standard.co.uk/insider/living/dog-and-cat-instagram-influencers-estimated-to-earn-as-much-as-32k-for-a-single-sponsored-post-a4317916.html

Leach, Edmund. 1989. Anthropological aspects of language: Animal categories and verbal abuse. *Anthrozoös*, 2(3): 151–165.

Leskin, Paige. 2019. The 22 most popular pet influencers, from Jiff Pom to Doug the Pug. *Insider*, 1 September. https://www.businessinsider.com/most-popular-pet-influencers-instagram-youtube-tiktok-jiff-pom-lil-bub-2019-8?r=US&IR=T

Lévi-Strauss, Claude. 1962. *The Savage Mind*. University of Chicago Press.

Morey, Darcy. 2010. *Dogs: Domestication and the Development of a Social Bond*. Cambridge University Press.

Ojoade, Olowo. 1990. Nigerian cultural attitudes to the dog. In *Signifying Animals: Human Meaning in the Natural World*, edited by Roy Wallis. Routledge, pp. 204–210.

PawTracks. 2020. The real reason cats randomly scratch people. *PawTracks*, 30 June. https://www.pawtracks.com/cats/why-cats-scratch-people/

Postrel, Virginia. 2018. Must love dogs? If you want the job. *Bloomberg Opinion*, 13 February. https://www.bloomberg.com/opinion/articles/2018-02-13/must-love-dogs-if-you-want-the-job

Radin, Paul. 1956. *The Trickster: A Study in American Indian Mythology*. Pantheon Books.

Sahlins, Marshall. 1978. *Culture and Practical Reason*. University of Chicago Press.

Statista. 2021. Average annual expenditure on dogs and cats in the United States as of 2020, by category. https://www.statista.com/statistics/250851/basic-annual-expenses-for-dog-and-cat-owners-in-the-us/

Tett, Gillian. 2021. *Anthro-Vision: How Anthropology Can Explain Business and Life*. Penguin Random House.

Tomkins, Silvan S. 2008. *Affect, Imagery, Consciousness*. Volume I & Volume II. Springer.

8. MENAGERIES AND STOCK MARKETS

Atherton, Mark. 2001. Market mumbo-jumbo explained. *The Times*, 24 March.

Fabozzi, Frank J. and Jack Clark Francis. 1977. Stability tests for alphas and betas over bull and bear market conditions. *Journal of Finance*, 32(4): 1093–1099.

FXCM. 2021. Bull market vs. bear market. *FXCM*, 15 December. https://www.fxcm.com/uk/insights/bull-market-vs-bear-market/

Gardner, Eriq. 2011. Harlan Ellison drops lawsuit claiming 'In Time' ripped off his story. *Hollywood Reporter*, 30 November. https://www.hollywoodreporter.com/business/business-news/in-time-harlan-ellison-lawsuit-dropped-267567/

Hanne, Jake Lee. 2017. The brutal bull-and-bear fights of 19th-century California. *Atlas Obscura*, 23 October. https://www.atlasobscura.com/articles/bull-and-bear-fights-california

Hall, Mary. 2021. Where did the bull and bear market get their names? *Investopedia*, 30 November. https://www.investopedia.com/ask/answers/bull-bear-market-names/

Indian Money. 2005. Etymology: History of the bull market and the bear market. *Indian Money*, 8 April. https://indianmoney.com/articles/etymology-history-of-bull-market-and-bear-market

Kahneman, Daniel and Jonathan Renshon. 2007. Why hawks win. *Foreign Policy*, Jan-Feb(158): 34–38.

Keynes, John Maynard. 2007. *The General Theory of Employment, Interest, and Money*. Palgrave Macmillan.

Lakoff, George and Mark Johnson. 1980. *Metaphors We Live By*. University of Chicago Press.

Lévi-Strauss, Claude. 1968. *The Savage Mind*. University of Chicago Press.

Life Financial Group. 2013. The bull vs. the bear. *Life Financial Group Blogspot*, 20 September. http://lifefinancialgroup.blogspot.com/2013/09/the-bull-vs-bear.html

Marx, Karl. 2004. *Capital: A Critique of Political Economy.* Volume I. Penguin.

Morris, Michael W., Oliver J. Sheldon, Daniel R. Ames, and Maia J. Young. 2007. Metaphors and the market: Consequences and preconditions of agent and object metaphors in stock market commentary. *Organizational Behavior & Human Decision Processes*, 102(2): 174–192.

Morris, William and Mary Morris. 1965. *Morris Dictionary of Words and Phrase Origins.* Harper Reference.

My2Sense. 2017. Actual footage of bull goring matador in butthole—11 inches deep. *YouTube*, 28 March. https://www.youtube.com/watch?v=TpWnhEGp9A8

Ritholtz, Barry. 2015. Stop thinking about markets as if they were human: your portfolio will do better if you do. *Bloomberg*, 28 July. https://www.bloomberg.com/opinion/articles/2015-07-28/stop-thinking-about-markets-as-if-they-were-human

Shah, Dhruti and Dominic Bailey. 2020. *Bear Markets and Beyond: A Bestiary of Business Terms.* Portico.

Sobel, Robert. 1965. *The Big Board: The History of the New York Stock Market.* Free Press.

Taleb, Nassim Nicholas. 2004. *Fooled by Randomness: The Hidden Role of Chance in Life and in the Markets.* Random House.

Tett, Gillian. 2021. *Anthro-Vision: How Anthropology Can Explain Business and Life.* Penguin Random House.

9. THE ILLOGIC OF TIPPING

Azer, Ofer H. 2004. The history of tipping—from sixteenth-century England to United States in the 1910s. *Journal of Socio-Economics*, 33(6): 745–764.

Biron, Bethany. 2021. Hooters adjusts policy to make controversial new uniform optional for employees after outcry over skimpy new shorts that are 'like underwear'. *Business Insider*, 17 October. https://www.businessinsider.com/hooters-adjusts-policy-to-make-con-troversial-new-shorts-optional-2021-10?r=US&IR=T

Burgess, John Frank. 2012. Tipping in Australia: The result of American influence? *Journal of Australian Studies*, 36(3): 377–392.

Cobble, Dorothy. 1992. *Dishing It Out: Waitresses and Their Unions in the Twentieth Century*. University of Illinois Press.

Foster, George M. 1972. The anatomy of envy: A study in symbolic behavior. *Current Anthropology*, 13(2): 165–202.

Fox, Kate. 2014. *Watching the English*. Second Edition. Hodder & Stoughton.

Ibbetson, Connor. 2020. Who, and how much, should you tip in Britain? *YouGov*, 30 June. https://yougov.co.uk/topics/economy/articles-reports/2020/06/30/who-and-how-much-should-you-tip-UK

Lynn, Michael. 1990. Determinants and consequences of female attractiveness and sexiness: Realistic tests with restaurant waitresses. *Archives of Sexual Behaviour*, 38: 737–745.

Mauss, Marcel. 1990. *The Gift: The Form and Reason for Exchange in Archaic Societies*. Routledge.

Murphy, Tim and CNT Editors. 2015. Etiquette 101: Your guide to tipping around the world. *Conde Nast Traveler*, 26 March. https://www.cntraveler.com/stories/2008-11-11/etiquette-101-tipping-guide

Nafiz, Hameda. 2022. Aussies are raging about being forced to tip after a meal out. *BuzzFeed*, 25 January. https://www.buzzfeed.com/haltherego/tipping-in-australia

Nestel, M.L. 2021. Short shrift: Hooters' new uniform change sparks fury from some waitresses as they brand skimpy short-shorts 'x-rated'. *The Sun*, 15 October. https://www.thesun.co.uk/news/16438035/hooters-uniform-fury-skimpy-short-shorts-x-rated/

Nguyen, Janet. 2021. How is digital tipping affecting

service workers? *Marketplace*, 18 June. https://www.
marketplace.org/2021/06/18/how-is-digital-tipping-af-
fecting-service-workers/

Pap, Leo. 1982. Tipping behavior as a semiotic process.
In *Semiotics 1980*, compiled by Michael Herzfeld and
Margot D. Lenhart. Plenum Press, pp. 373–382.

Scott, William R. 1916. *The Itching Palm: A Study of the Habit
of Tipping in America*. Paducah.

Segrave, Kerry. 1998. *Tipping: An American Social History of
Gratuities*. McFarland & Company.

Shamir, Boas. 1984. Between gratitude and gratuity: An
analysis of tipping. *Annals of Tourism Research*, 11: 59–78.

Swanson, Ana. 2015. There's a scientific reason why New
Year's Eve is generally terrible. *The Washington Post*, 31
December. https://www.washingtonpost.com/news/
wonk/wp/2015/12/31/theres-a-scientific-reason-new-
years-eve-is-generally-terrible/

SuesyQ_11. 2016. Tipping in Australia. Please don't
tip!!!!! *Tripadvisor.co.uk*. https://www.tripadvisor.co.uk/
ShowTopic-g255055-i120-k9340842-Tipping_in_Aus-
tralia_Please_Don_t_Tip-Australia.html

Wee, Heesun. 2016. More restaurants opting for no-tip
policies: Survey. *CNBC*, 2 June. https://www.cnbc.
com/2016/06/02/more-restaurants-opting-for-no-tip-
policies-survey.html

Zelizer, Viviana. 1999. *The Social Meaning of Money*. Perseus
Books.

10. BEWARE OF COLLEAGUES BEARING DRINKS

Carrier, James. 1990. Gifts in a world of commodities: the
ideology of the perfect gift in American society. *Social
Analysis*, 29: 19–37.

Carrier, James. 1991. Gifts, commodities, and social relations: A Maussian view of exchange. *Sociological Forum*,
6(1): 119-136.

Cornell, Martyn. 2018. So what IS the difference between

a pub and a bar? *Zythophile*. 12 August. https://zytho-phile.co.uk/2018/12/08/so-what-is-the-difference-be-tween-a-pub-and-a-bar/

Douglas, Mary. 1990. Foreword. In *The Gift: The Form and Reason for Exchange in Archaic Societies*, by Marcel Mauss. Routledge, pp. ix–xxiii.

Fitzsimmons, Caitlin. 2017. Buying rounds is deeply ingrained in Aussie culture but widely disliked. *Sydney Morning Herald*, 1 September. https://www.smh.com.au/money/saving/buying-rounds-is-deeply-engrained-in-aussie-culture-but-widely-disliked-20170901-gy971p.html

Fox, Kate. 2014. *Watching the English*. Second Edition. Hodder & Stoughton.

Harper, Douglas. 2002. Treat. *Online Etymology Dictionary*. https://www.etymonline.com/search?q=treat

Kapferer, Bruce. 1988. *Legends of People, Myths of State: Violence, Intolerance, and Political Culture in Sri Lanka and Australia*. Crawford House Publishing.

Marshall, Nikki and Anna Livsley. 2017. No hands, ma'am: Australian prime ministers meet the Queen, in pictures. *The Guardian*, 12 July. https://www.theguardian.com/australia-news/gallery/2017/jul/12/no-hands-maam-australian-prime-ministers-meet-the-queen-in-pictures

Mauss, Marcel. 1990. *The Gift: The Form and Reason for Exchange in Archaic Societies*. Routledge.

McCammon, Ross. 2010. How to buy a round for everyone in the bar. *Esquire*, 20 August. https://www.esquire.com/food-drink/food/how-to/a8273/how-to-buy-a-round-082010/

Sahlins, Marshall. 1972. *Stone Age Economics*. Aldine.

Sedaris, David. 2020. Christmas means giving. In *The Best of Me*. Abacus.

Staff Writers. 2022. From the archives, 1992: British tabloids incensed by 'Lizard of Oz'. *The Age*, 23 February.

https://www.theage.com.au/national/from-the-ar-
chives-1992-british-tabloids-incensed-by-lizard-of-oz-
20220217-p59xez.html

Tett, Gillian. 2021. *Anthro-Vision: How Anthropology Can Explain Business and Life.* Penguin Random House.

Wikiquote. 2021. Bono. https://en.wikiquote.org/wiki/Bono

Wierzbicka, Anna. 1997. *Understanding Cultures Through Their Key Words: English, Russian, Polish, German, and Japanese.* Oxford University Press.

11. YOU CAN'T SAY 'C*NT' IN CANADA

Adams, Sam. 2013. The 'c-word' is cordial: Edgar Wright, 'The World's End' and the British censors. *IndieWire*, 31 July. https://www.indiewire.com/2013/07/the-c-word-is-cordial-edgar-wright-the-worlds-end-and-the-british-censors-127615/

Allan, Keith and Kate Burridge. 2006. *Forbidden Words: Taboo and the Censoring of Language.* Cambridge University Press.

Barley, Nigel. 1983. *The Innocent Anthropologist: Notes from a Mud Hut.* Waveland Press.

Beers Fägersten, Kristy and Karyn Stapleton, editors. 2017. Introduction: Swearing research as variations on a theme. In *Advances in Swearing Research: New Languages and New Contexts.* John Benjamins Publishing Company, pp. 1–15.

Beirne, Piers. 2020. Animals, women and terms of abuse: Towards a cultural etymology of con(e)y, cunny, cunt and c*nt. *Critical Criminology*, 28: 327–349.

Billington, Alex. 2013. This is how it should work: 'The World's End' letter from the censor. *Firstshowing.net*, 1 August. https://www.firstshowing.net/2013/this-is-how-it-should-work-the-worlds-end-letter-from-the-censor/

Burridge, Kate. 2016. The 'c-word' may be the last

swearing taboo, but doesn't shock like it used to. *The Conversation*, 17 February. https://theconversation.com/the-c-word-may-be-the-last-swearing-taboo-but-doesnt-shock-like-it-used-to-54813

Bryson, Bill. 1990. *The Mother Tongue: English and How it Got That Way*. Avon Books.

Byrd, Matthew. 2018. Ready Player One's f-bomb is one of the best ever. *Den of Geek*, 2 April. https://www.denofgeek.com/movies/ready-player-ones-f-bomb-is-one-of-the-best-ever/

Byrne, Emma. 2017. *Swearing is Good for You: The Amazing Science of Bad Language*. W.W. Norton & Company.

Douglas, Mary. 2003. *Purity and Danger: An Analysis of the Concepts of Pollution and Taboo*. Routledge.

Esposito, Brad. 2014. 9 outrageous words that are said every day in Australia. *BuzzFeed*, 20 February. https://www.buzzfeed.com/bradesposito/outrageous-words-that-are-said-every-day-in-australia

Finkelstein, Shlomit Ritz. 2018. Swearing and the brain. In *Oxford Handbook of Taboo Words and Language*, edited by Keith Allan. Oxford University Press, pp. 108–139.

Fox, Kate. 2014. *Watching the English*. Second Edition. Hodder & Stoughton.

Gardener, R. Allen, Beatrix T. Gardner, and Thomas E. Van Cantfort. 1989. *Teaching Sign Language to Chimpanzees*. State University of New York Press.

Gauthier, Michael and Adrien Guille. 2017. Gender and age differences in swearing. A corpus study of Twitter. In *Advances in Swearing Research: New Languages and New Contexts*, edited by Kristy Beers Fägersten and Karyn Stapleton. John Benjamins Publishing Company, pp. 137–156.

Greer, Germaine. 1970. *The Female Eunuch*. MacGibbon & Kee.

Hall of Advertising. 2019. Toyota Hilux—Bugger (1999, New Zealand). *YouTube*, 14 July. https://www.youtube.

com/watch?v=ZUNJd06iyWU

Hughes, Geoffrey. 1991. *Swearing: A Social History of Foul Language, Oaths and Profanity in English.* Penguin.

Hughes, Geoffrey. 2015. *An Encyclopedia of Swearing: The Social History of Oaths, Profanity, Foul Language, and Ethnic Slurs in the English-Speaking World.* Routledge.

Lakoff, Robin. 1975. *Language and Women's Place.* Harper Collins.

Laugesen, Amanda. 2020. *Rooted: An Australian History of Bad Language.* NewSouth Publishing.

Leach, Edmund. 1989. Anthropological aspects of language: Animal categories and verbal abuse. *Anthrozoös,* 2(3): 151–165.

Maynard, Senko K. 1997. *Japanese Communication: Language and Thought in Context.* University of Hawaii Press.

McKelle, Erin. 2016. Why I think it's important to reclaim the word 'c*nt'. *Ravishly,* 13 May. https://ravishly.com/2016/12/28/why-i-think-its-important-reclaim-word-cnt

McLaughlin, Robert J. 1981. Language and man: Aristotle meets Koko. *Thomist: A Speculative Quarterly Review,* 45(4): 451–470.

Montagu, Ashley. 1967. *The Anatomy of Swearing.* University of Pennsylvania Press.

Outback Dictionary. 2022. 'Cunt' meaning. https://outbackdictionary.com/cunt/

Quora. 2022. How offensive is the word 'cunt' in Australia? https://www.quora.com/How-offensive-is-the-word-%E2%80%9Ccunt%E2%80%9D-in-Australia

Reductress. 2021. How I reclaimed the word 'cunt' by being one. Reductress, 1 June. *https://reductress.com/post/how-i-reclaimed-the-word-cunt-by-being-one/*

Sheidlower, Jesse. 1999. *The F-Word.* Random House.

Wierzbicka, Anna. 1997. *Understanding Cultures Through Their Key Words: English, Russian, Polish, German, and Japanese.* Oxford University Press.

12. CACK HANDS AND SOUTHPAWS

Bishop D.V.M. 1990. On the futility of using familial sinistrality to subclassify handedness groups. *Cortex*, 26: 153–155.

Cashmore, Lisa, Natalie Uomini, and Amandine Chapelain. 2008. The evolution of handedness in humans and great apes: a review and current issues. *Journal of Anthropological Sciences*, 86: 7–35.

Dowling, Tim. 2015. Knives out for British table manners. *The Guardian*, 19 October. https://www.theguardian.com/lifeandstyle/shortcuts/2015/oct/19/knives-out-table-manners-american-style-fork-switching

Fitch, W. Tecumseh and Stephanie N. Braccini. 2013. Primate laterality and the biology and evolution of human handedness: a review and synthesis. *Annals of the New York Academy of Sciences*, 1288: 70–85.

Harris, Lauren Julius. 2010. In fencing, what gives left-handers the edge? Views from the present and the distant past. *Laterality: Asymmetries of Brain, Behaviour, and Cognition*, 15(1/2): 15-55.

Hertz, Robert. 2013. The pre-eminence of the right hand: A study in religious polarity. *Hau: Journal of Ethnographic Theory*, 3(2): 335–357.

Hodgson, Geoffrey M. 2018. *Wrong Turnings: How the Left Got Lost.* University of Chicago Press.

Kishore, Praveen. 2019. How do Indians clean their bottoms? *Fair Observer*, 29 May. https://www.fairobserver.com/region/central_south_asia/indian-bathroom-etiquette-hygiene-shattaf-bidet-shower-asian-news-90482/

Lee, Seo-young. 2017. The world that 88% are unaware of. *Korea Times*, 9 September. https://www.koreatimes.co.kr/www/nation/2017/08/181_234434.html

Liberman, Anatoly. 2010. The sinister influence of the left hand. *Oxford University Press Blog*, 22 September. https://blog.oup.com/2010/09/left-hand/

Llaurens, V., M. Raymond, and C. Faurie. 2009. Why are some people left-handed? An evolutionary perspective. *Philosophical Transactions of the Royal Society B*, 364: 881–894.

Marchant, Linda F. and W.C. McCrew. 1998. Human handedness: An ethological perspective. *Human Evolution*, 13: 221–228.

Needham, Rodney, editor. 1973. *Right and Left: Essays on Dual Symbolic Classification.* University of Chicago Press.

Oldfield, R.C. 1971. The assessment and analysis of handedness: The Edinburgh Inventory. *Neuropsychologica*, 9: 97–113.

Papadatou-Pastou, Marietta. 2011. Handedness and language lateralization: why are we right-handed and left-brained? *Hellenic Journal of Psychology*, 8: 248–265.

Pfeifer, Lena Sophie, Judith Schmitz, Mariette Papadatou-Pastou, Jutta Peterburs, Silvia Paracchini, and Sebastian Ocklenburg. 2022. Handedness in twins: Meta-analysis. *BMC Psychology*, 10(11).

Raymond, M. and D. Pontier. 2004. Is there geographical variation in human handedness? *Laterality: Asymmetries of Brain, Behaviour, and Cognition*, 9(1): 35–51.

Rodway, Paul, Volker Thoma and Astrid Schepman. 2022. The effects of sex and handedness on masturbation laterality and other lateralized motor behaviours. *Laterality: Asymmetries of Brain, Behaviour, and Cognition*, 27(3): 324–352.

Schott, G.D. 2007. Mirror writing: Neurological reflections on an unusual phenomenon. *Journal of Neurology, Neurosurgery & Psychiatry*, 78(1): 5–13.

Sicotte, Nancy L., Roger P. Woods, and John C. Mazziotta. 1999. Handedness in twins: A meta-analysis. *Laterality: Asymmetries of Body, Brain and Cognition*, 4(3): 265–286.

Usher, Tom. 2016. We asked a sex therapist about the thrills of left-handed wanking. *Vice*, 13 August.

https://www.vice.com/en/article/xdmxbq/ask-expert-left-handed-masturbation

13. THE MAGIC OF NUMBERS

Basketball Noise. 2021. What jersey number did Michael Jordan wear? https://basketballnoise.com/what-jersey-number-did-michael-jordan-wear/

Chalabi, Mona. 2014. Words you can write on a calculator. *The Guardian*, 10 January. https://www.theguardian.com/education/datablog/2014/jan/10/words-you-can-write-on-a-calculator

Crump, Thomas. 1990. *The Anthropology of Numbers*. Cambridge University Press.

Douglas, Mary. 2003. *Purity and Danger: An Analysis of the Concepts of Pollution and Taboo*. Routledge.

Fortin, Nicole M., Andrew J. Hill, and Jeff Huang. 2013. Superstition in the housing market. *IZA Discussion Paper Series*, No. 7484.

Frazer, James G. 2013. *The Golden Bough*. Third Edition. Cambridge University Press.

Goal. 2021. Why does Cristiano Ronaldo wear the no. 7 shirt? *Goal*, 6 September. https://www.goal.com/en-us/news/why-does-cristiano-ronaldo-wear-the-no7-shirt/ogsfw81ff0lw1dr4ih2jitj2c

Gmelch, George. 2000. Baseball magic. In *Through the Looking Glass: Readings in Anthropology*, edited by Lee Cronk and Vaughn M. Bryant, Jr. Second Edition. McGraw-Hill, pp. 1–5.

Harper, Douglas. 2022. Odd. *Online Etymology Dictionary*. https://www.etymonline.com/word/odd#etymonline_v_2492

Haeffner, Mark. 2004. *Dictionary of Alchemy: From Maria Prophetessa to Isaac Newton*. Aeon Books.

Harris, Nick. 2007. Bad omen for Italy as their unlucky number comes up. *Independent*, 15 November. https://www.independent.co.uk/sport/football/european/

bad-omen-for-italy-as-their-unlucky-number-comes-up-400380.html

Hayward, Justin. 2021. Why most airlines don't have a row 13 on their planes. *Simple Flying*, 2 April. https://simpleflying.com/row-13-on-planes/

Humble, Steve. 2016. Why '7' is the luckiest number. *The Conversation*, 8 March. https://theconversation.com/why-7-is-the-luckiest-number-55960

Humphreys, Brad R., Adam Nowak, and Yang Zhou. 2019. Superstition and real estate prices: Transaction-level evidence from the US housing market. *Applied Economics*, 51(26); 2818–2841.

Malinowski, Bronislaw. 1948. *Magic, Science and Religion and Other Essays*. Waveland Press.

May, Sam. 2020. Cristiano Ronaldo: Why is the no. 7 jersey so important to him? *Forbes*, 10 February. https://www.forbes.com/sites/sammay/2020/02/10/cristiano-ronaldo-why-is-the-no7-jersey-so-important-to-him/

Ng, Travis, Terence Chong, and Xin Du. 2010. The value of superstitions. *Journal of Economic Psychology*, 31: 293-309.

Ore, Oystein. 1948. *Number Theory and Its History*. Dover Publications, Inc.

Orwell, George. 1950. *1984*. Penguin Classics.

Perkins, Broderick. 2002. Bottom line conjures up realty's fear of 13. *Realty Times*, 13 September. https://web.archive.org/web/20130430013751/http://realtytimes.com/rtpages/20020913_13thfloor.htm

Phillips, David A. 1992. *Numerology: Discovering the Inner Self*. Hay House.

Pratchett, Terry and Neil Gaiman. 1990. *Good Omens*. Corgi.

Rogerson, Barnaby. 2013. *Rogerson's Book of Numbers*. Profile Books.

Schimmel, Annemarie. 1993. *The Mystery of Numbers*. Oxford University Press.

Taleb, Nassim Nicholas. 2004. *Fooled by Randomness: The Hidden Role of Chance in Life and in the Markets.* Random House.

Thompson, Tok. 2002. The thirteenth number: Then, there/here and now. *Studia Mythologica Slavica,* V: 145–160.

Watkins, Matthew. 2015. *Secrets of Creation Volume 1: The Mystery of Prime Numbers.* Liberalis.

Wiseman, Richard. 2007. *Quirkology: The Curious Science of Everyday Lives.* Pan Books.

CONCLUSION

Adshead, Samuel Adrian Miles. 1992. *Salt and Civilization.* Palgrave.

Alarco, Jose and Peter Talbot. 2015. Charged up: the history and development of batteries. *The Conversation,* 30 April. https://theconversation.com/charged-up-the-history-and-development-of-batteries-40372

English Language & Usage. 2022. Is the etymology of 'salary' a myth? https://english.stackexchange.com/questions/448865/is-the-etymology-of-salary-a-myth

Gladwell, Malcolm. 2005. *Blink: The Power of Thinking Without Thinking.* Little, Brown & Company.

History Extra. 2022. Why do we say 'with a pinch of salt'? https://www.historyextra.com/period/roman/who-do-we-say-with-a-pinch-of-salt/

Martin, Gary. 2022. Take it with a grain of salt. *The Phrase Finder.* https://www.phrases.org.uk/meanings/take-with-a-grain-of-salt.html

Mintz, Sidney W. 1986. *Sweetness and Power: The Place of Sugar in Modern History.* Penguin Books.

Rittenhouse, Madison. 2020. Brazilian slang: 8 food idioms every Portuguese learner must learn. *Pimsleur Language Blog,* 13 November. https://blog.pimsleur.com/2020/11/13/brazilian-food-idioms-slang/ Ritz,

Eberhard. 2006. Salt—friend or foe? Nephrology Dialysis Transplantation, 21: 2052-2056.

Schmeck Jr, Harold M. 1983. Hunger for salt found to be powerful instinct. *New York Times*, 9 August. https://www.nytimes.com/1983/08/09/science/hunger-for-salt-found-to-be-powerful-instinct.html

Tett, Gillian. 2021. *Anthro-Vision: How Anthropology Can Explain Business and Life.* Penguin Random House.

Young, Liam Cole. 2020. Salt: Fragments from the history of a medium. *Theory, Culture & Society,* 37(6): 135-158.

Illustrations

Acknowledgements

It is usual practice to suggest in acknowledgements that it takes a village to write a book, but that's a polite lie. It takes one person to write a book, but it takes a village to make it publishable—a village full of recalcitrant villagers, who must be mercilessly bullied and endlessly harangued into giving feedback on chapters. In other words, it's your classic troll-villager relationship, with the troll demanding acts of fealty from the villagers and howling outside their houses every night until they fold.

First and foremost, I must acknowledge my family, a.k.a. those I bullied the most. My sister, Nikki Adshead-Bell, read every chapter, but was unstinting in her praise, so I knew her opinion couldn't be trusted. My mother, Sue, was likewise too prejudiced in my favour to be reliable. I wanted honest feedback, damnit!—but only so long as they loved what they read. My brother, Chris, read half a chapter but told me he'd wait for the book (it's here, Chris, so you've got no more excuses). Neil Adshead, my brother-in-law, a more reliable and impartial sounding bound, was also cajoled into giving feedback on several chapters—you can blame him for the one on swearing, which he suggested.

My father, Tim, on the other hand, was initially very sceptical about this book. A retired academic geologist, he saw little point in writing a non-academic book, when that time would be better spent on papers—at least three could surely be written in the time it would take me to finish a book! But he eventually came around. In fact, I had to give him a stern talking to at one point, because every left-hander he met was foisted with a copy of 'Cack Hands and Southpaws', whether they wanted it or not. 'Stop giving my chapter to random strangers!' I scolded him. In the end, he read every chapter, providing pithy, albeit vague, assessments. 'Quite superb. Needs nothing', was the verdict on one. 'Not as good or as fun or as interesting as the others', he wrote of another.

But the person I owe the greatest debt to is my husband, Andrew Ham. Yes, he wasn't thrilled at being featured in several chapters. Yes, he had to be threatened, cajoled, and blackmailed into reading the book. Yes, his blunt honesty wasn't always appreciated ('You're being ridiculous', he told me, after I dramatically declared that I was giving up on the book following some mild criticism on his part). But he was very supportive of me writing it, and was its biggest fan in the end. Like my dad, he, too, started foisting copies of chapters on co-workers, although Mike Wrotniak's feedback helped convince me that someone who wasn't related to me might actually find the book interesting.

Many of Andrew's colleagues also had the misfortune to be in my vicinity at a recent wedding when I was deep in the throes of the book. Kara Hobbs was grilled about buying drinks in the USA while we drank them at the reception; Mike Barton briefed me on the differences between kitchens, pantries, and sculleries when I abruptly turned the dinner conversation to washing machines; and John Sisay was forced to listen to me raving about the word 'cunt' for literally hours on end during the car trip up to Northampton (although I think he fell asleep in self-defence).

Naturally, my colleagues weren't let off the hook either—why on earth would I waste all that free proximal expertise? Nadine Beckmann, Colette Berbesque, Harry Marshall, Todd C. Rae, Caroline Ross, and Stuart Semple were all arm-twisted into giving feedback on chapters. Other colleagues contributed indirectly (and unwittingly) through vociferous lunchtime debates on several of the topics discussed in the book: Volker Behrends, Lia Betti, Julia Lehmann, Garry Marvin, Isabel Santos Magalhaes, Allan McElligott, Istvan Praet, Julia Reiss, Anne Robertson, and Peter Shaw (although you need to move on from slugs and snails, guys, because I won).

Other friends and colleagues who have contributed to this book in one way or another include Darlene McNaughton, Ciara Kierans, Svetlana Ristovski-Slijepcevic, Shaylih Muehlmann, Sally McBeth, and Jovan Maud. I also want to acknowledge the influence of my core teachers and mentors at James Cook University: Rosita Henry, Douglas Miles (now sadly deceased), Rohan Bastin, and my doctoral supervisor, Bruce Kapferer, to whom this book is dedicated (a dubious honour, it must be said). I am also grateful to the feedback from the postgraduate students who read a draft of 'Laundry Location, Location, Location' as part of a University of Roehampton writing workshop, especially Åsa Melander.

Because I fear that my strategy of naming people to obligate them to buy the book is becoming a little too transparent, I will wrap things up here, but in closing I want to acknowledge my copy editor Sandy Draper, and

Erin Taylor and the *Popanth* crew. *Popanth* published the original versions of 'Silent but Deadly', 'Must Love Dogs', and 'The Illogic of Tipping' and I benefited from the lively discussion they generated. An abbreviated version of 'Going to the Dentist Bites' was also published in *The Globe & Mail* in 2009 and 'A Slug is a Snail Without a House' was published on the *Anthroehampton* blog in 2018. Although all pieces have been greatly expanded, they are reproduced here with permission.

Kirsten Bell is the UK's pre-eminent female Australian anthropologist born in 1975.* She received her doctorate in social anthropology from James Cook University in Australia in 2000 and is currently a visiting professor at King's College London. She has previously held appointments at the University of Northern Colorado, Macquarie University, the University of British Columbia, and the University of Roehampton, where she was Professor of Social Anthropology. To learn more about Kirsten and her work, visit her website at www.notkristenbell.com.

*She has no means of substantiating this claim but how many of us can there be?

Printed in Great Britain
by Amazon

10399381R00131